City Fields,
Country Gardens

City Fields, Country Gardens

Michael Hyde

Edited and introduced by
David Crouch and Martin Stott

Five Leaves Publications

City Fields, Country Gardens

Published in 1998 by Five Leaves Publications,
PO Box 81, Nottingham NG5 4ER, Great Britain

Five Leaves acknowledges financial support from
East Midlands Arts

EAST
MIDLANDS
ARTS

Photographs taken on allotment sites
in England and France in 1990 and 1994.
Cover photograph: Scarecrow, Elderstubbs Site, Oxford

Printed in Great Britain by Antony Rowe
Design by 4 Sheets Design

ISBN 0 907123 72 4

This blessed plot,
this earth,
this realm...
Shakespeare, King Richard II

Contents

Introduction	**i**
Breaking Ground	**1**
Blessed Plot	3
Inspirations	**5**
Miller's Tale	7
The Testament of a Grand Old Gardener	9
Under the Gooseberry Bush	12
Place for Women	15
Women's Realm	17
Living Canvas by Bumps	19
Prickly Producer	22
Going Back to Our Roots	24
Freedom to Potter	27
Rusticated to a Fertile Plot	29
How to Hatch a Plot	30
Holding Your Ground	**33**
Gardening for Leisure	35
The Amateurs and the Clod Bashers	37
Altruistic Toil	39
Allotments in Demand	42
The Price of a Plot Thickens	45
Lords and Others	48
Rabbits	51
The Plot, the Law, and the Class Factor	54
Plotting for the Good Life	57
The Shape of Things to Come	60
A Good Plot Wears Thin	63
Sod's Law	65

Culture   67
Ground Rules   69
Breath of Fresh Air   72
Gardener's Weather   75
A Place for Children   78
Seed Saving   81
Rubbish Recycled   84
Carry on Mulching   86
Dutch Light   89
Weeding for the Weak-kneed   91
Getting to Grips with the Mole   93
Soft Fruit and Feathered Friends   96
Nelson Puts a Good Eye to the Glass   98
Clearing Winter Cupboards   100

The Worm and the Earth   103
Red in Tooth and Claw   105
The Worm Turns   107
Family Friends   110
Relying on a Bed of Nettles   113
A Harvest of Hedgehogs   115
Do You Know Your Enemies?   118
In Praise of English Apples   121

Plant Listing   125
A Ripe Time for Rejoicing   127
You Don't Have to Provide Umbrellas   130
Cheering Wine and Pan Pipes   132
The Plot Thickets   134
Strawberry Fields   137
Coming Up Rosy   140
It's a Good Old Bean   142
Allotment Wines   145
In Praise of the Noble Spud   148
Cabbages in Depth   151
Corn on the Compost   153
Artichoke Pie   156
Pepper Proud   158

Harvest of Love Apples 160
Miracle Comfrey 163
Woad Show 165
Garlic 168
Rootful Abundance 171
Parsley: The Good Companion 174
Allotment Tipples 176

All in the End is Harvest? **179**
This Blessed Plot 181
Plot Bound No More 183

Introduction

Not (only) writing but digging

Allotments are currently in the news again, but Michael
Hyde paved the way with a monthly allotment column in
the *Guardian* over a twenty five year period. As well as
being a listing of garden-tips, the column connected a wide
world of history, sustainability, allotment struggles and
food campaigns. There was also a lot of humour and rich
anecdote.

In this book, culled from all those articles, we have tried
to portray something of the colour and diversity of what
Michael Hyde wrote. In this introduction we hope not to
swamp the book with our enthusiasm, but connect his
work to what has happened to allotments since he began
writing. We identify his contribution to the allotment
story and in the spirit of Michael's writing, we make
connections to the wider world which, with Michael, we
believe the humble plot has always had. And is likely to
continue to have, with renewed vigour, in the future. We
make a brief sketch of Michael's life, how he emerged into
an enthusiasm for allotments. Not only writing but
digging.

The book is divided into sections, reflecting those areas
of writing that Hyde particularly loved — for example
historical reference and inspirations towards having and
keeping an allotment. We have included the richness of his
commentary on growing and nurturing and on cultivation,
because here again he transcended the traditional
approach of garden-tips, by making numerous connections
in time and place.

Though the collection is presented in sections for ease of
approach, Hyde's writing is too rich to be bound in this
way. Thus, in the same section you are likely to find
stories from Holland, Japan, or China in Tudor times.

Hyde publicised an allotment profile which embraced all allotment holders (though especially *Guardian* reading ones) and a wide range of organisations active in the field — the Soil Association, the Henry Doubleday Research Association, the National Society of Allotment and Leisure Gardeners and many more. He thus helped create an informal network of groups with diverse constituencies but overlapping interests.

Michael Hyde himself was born in 1908 in Shipton-under-Wychwood and raised in the nearby village of Wootton, Oxfordshire, where his father was a servant in the local "big house". After the First World War the family moved to Yorkshire where he won a scholarship to Malton Grammar School. This was on the strength of being able to spell "separate", acquired from his daily operation of the milk separator on his uncle's farm. Almost inevitably he became a schoolmaster, but wartime soldiering in North Italy aroused his interest in intensive horticulture. The appearance of his first gardening article in the airmail edition of the *Guardian* launched him on his subsequent career as a writer, mostly of scripts for the BBC School Broadcasting Department, but also of plays and stories about Arctic whaling.

Retiring to the edge of the Yorkshire Wolds, he intended to devote himself to writing but instead took on an a neglected allotment, and — as they say in those parts — got topside of it. Hyde began his regular column in the *Guardian* in 1968.

Michael Hyde wrote about the growth of the environmental and green movements. And though he wrote often about garden history he was not sucked in to false nostalgia for a mythical past.

His column emerged just at the time the Government enquiry into allotments, the *Thorpe Report* of 1969, was published. Thorpe argued for a more designer style approach to allotment sites — "leisure gardens" — to save them. In the event, in the succeeding decade the determination of the new movements associated with the environment, with safe food and with urban wildlife, preserved the vernacular architecture of allotment sheds from being "tidied away". Nevertheless Thorpe enabled the allotment world to recover its popularity and public face. With the 70s, local authorities, the main owners of allotment land, found an increased demand for sites and plots. The *Guardian* may be considered brave for being the only national newspaper to publish Hyde's column for another quarter of a century.

We complete this collection as another wave of allotment interest surrounds us. There have been a number of television films on allotment life.[1] There is a resurgence of allotment photography and other artwork. Poetry too![2] As we write, a six month long exhibition of allotment life and history opens at the Pump House Peoples History Museum in Manchester. *Amateur Gardening*'s Allotments 2000 campaign has attracted attention to the threats posed to allotments. *The Big Issue* has had a feature on allotment campaigners, the new magazine *The Kitchen Garden* has an allotment section. The subject has even reached the IKEA magazine, *Room,* and the *Sunday Telegraph* now has an allotment column. This summer too, an intervention artist, Harry Palmer, is working with plotholders in three allotment sites turning a further fresh eye onto the plot.

Recent research[3] demonstrates the scale of the decline in allotment provision. From 1.5 million plots at the end of World War II, numbers have declined to little over a quarter of a million now, while the number of vacant plots rise and waiting lists decline. The trend has been for sites that are not protected by statute, ie "temporary" and private sites, to be disposed of. The result is that in the last twenty years the number of statutory sites has risen from around half to over three-quarters of the total available.[4] While this trend is discouraging, the reason for plots being vacant are concealed — with the resulting temptation to dispose of them. Plots get, and stay, empty because the sites are poorly managed or have poor security. The vacancies are not usually in the same places there are waiting lists. Councils may not advertise availability. There is evidence that enthusiastic allotment associations attract new people in.

Allotments, though under pressure,[5] have come to occupy many corners of contemporary life. Gardening as a whole continues to be the most popular leisure pursuit in Britain, despite a wider spectrum of alternatives than ever before. There is a changing face of gardening, more commercially in tune with popular culture, as the shift of plant buying from nursery to garden centre demonstrates, as does the popularity of gardening magazines and programmes on television. Though this has brought strimmers to the allotment, and parked cars where once were bicycles, the character of allotment pleasure remains. Allotments bring deferred rewards rather than immediate gain. Care and cultivation remain predominant — seasoned with emotion and friendship.

Food grown on allotments may not have what we have come to know as "supermarket quality". Allotment food is not sprayed for appearance. As well as being safer, tastier and cheaper, allotment food looks like real food, complete with knobbly bits and irregular shapes. Allotment food avoids the "food miles", which may bring asparagus from Peru or mangetout from Zimbabwe, but at an environmental cost — not least in the fuel used to get the goods to your supermarket.

Government policy announcements that 60% of the 4.4 million new houses to be built in the 25 years to 2016 should be built on "brownfield" sites in urban areas will mean that new homes will have smaller gardens or, as flats, be carved out of redundant industrial buildings. These are powerful reasons why city allotment sites should be retained. They break up the urban landscape, and help in providing the urban green lungs we need to keep the cities alive, and to provide a refuge for urban wildlife. Allotment sites provide democratic and cheap access to gardening and food growing.[6]

The Government is currently considering its view in the light of the House of Commons Environment Select Committee Inquiry on the future of allotments. Both of us have given evidence on the value of allotment life.[7] We argued that building on allotments is exactly the wrong thing to do. We don't want to have to invent groups like New York's Green Guerillas, marvellous as they are in bringing greenery and life to otherwise concrete streets.

As campaigners for allotments, we, and our publisher, hope Michael Hyde's book will be enjoyed by those who remember the articles, those who are fresh to allotment life and by those in public life whose decisions matter.

Finally a few notes on the *dramatis personae* of the text.

Nelson, who is mentioned a number of times, was Hyde's very good friend and neighbouring octogenarian plotholder. The late Lawrence Hills was the creator and driving force of the Henry Doubleday Research Association, which promotes and investigates organic cultivation. Their headquarters and demonstration site is now at Ryton on Dunsmore, Coventry, CV8 3LG. The late Tom Hume led the London Association of Recreational Gardeners (LARG) over three decades. The LARG were concerned, at the time, about a perceived lack of action by the main allotment group, the National Society of Allotment and Leisure Gardeners. The National Society now represents many tens of thousands of allotment holders and gives voice to the movement. They can be contacted at NSALG Office, O'Dell House, Hunter's Road, Corby, Northants. Harry Thorpe, Professor of Geography at Birmingham University is known for his leadership of the *Inquiry into Allotments,* affectionately known as the *Thorpe Report.* He worked with Elizabeth Galloway on allotment rationalisation schemes for Birmingham City Council, which used the word correctly, making good use of allotment land rather than *rationalising* it away.

The other players in the allotment book — Jane and John Loudon, Gertrude Jekyll, Nicholas Culpepper, John Gerrard, Capability Brown, Sydney Smith, John Clare,

Gerrard Winstanley and others were not allotmenters but gardeners, herbalists, designers, poets and revolutionaries. We leave the reader to chase up these historical figures at will.

David Crouch and Martin Stott
May, 1998

[1] *The Plot* (David Crouch/Ray Hough, BBC2, 1994), *The Woman's Plot* (Amanda Richardson, BBC2, 1993), *The Ballad of the Ten Rod Plot* (Richard Deakin, ITV, 1993) and *Vegetable Plots* (Taghi Amarani/David Crouch, Channel Four, 1992).

[2] See, for example, the title poem of *Lifting the Language* by Sue Dymoke (Shoestring, 1998).

[3] *The 1997 Report on the Survey of Allotments in England,* by David Crouch, was published by the National Society in association with Anglia University. Copies are available from the National Society. There are currently 296,923 allotments in England, covering 25,416 acres. 43,584 plots are vacant. 12,950 people are on waiting lists. Details for Wales, Scotland and Northern Ireland are as yet unavailable. An earlier survey for the National Society showed that the age range of allotment holders was spread evenly between the mid-thirties and the retired, and that the proportion of women plotholders had increased from only 3% 30 years ago to 15% in 1997.

[4] Allotment legislation is most marked by The Allotment Act of 1908 which legislated that local councils had to provide allotments to those who need them, if at least five local citizens on the electoral register so request. Subsequent legislation stopped the requirement that allotments were limited to the "labouring poor" and that land bought for allotments by a local council cannot be converted to any other use without Ministerial (now Secretary of State) approval. These are the so-called Statutory sites. The Allotment Act of 1950 enigmatically said that plot rents must be such as a tenant may reasonably be expected to pay. A subsequent, but failed bill (the Recreational Gardening Bill of 1986) tried to establish that allotments were recreation rather than agricultural/horticultural in the hope of bringing allotments more into the mainstream of local

authority funded recreation. Of course those who understand allotments know that they are profoundly a recreation which included growing food.

[5] In the most recent edition of *The Allotment: Its Landscape and Culture,* by David Crouch and Colin Ward (Five Leaves, 1997), there is mention of the historic Town Moor site being under threat by Newcastle United wishing to develop a new stadium on the site. The future of this case is uncertain.

[6] Readers may wish to consult *Growing Food in Cities* (available from the National Food Alliance and SAFE, 11 Worship Street, London EC1A 2BH). This report shows new, imaginative and inventive ways to organise to grow food and opens up allotments to a wider, very active and inclusive future.

[7] Environment Transport and Regional Affairs Committee: The Future for Allotments June 1998.

Breaking
Ground

Blessed Plot

When you have suffered land-hunger for sixty years it is time to do something about it, and particularly so if you know of some council allotments in open country where the larks sing.

This was the argument I presented, some weeks ago, to myself, but not my wife. She declared that digging, in my case, was very unwise. She was against it entirely.

But there are times when a man suffering from land-hunger must assert himself, and override all opposition. What is the use of those BBC gardeners telling you how to get rid of couch grass, if you have no couch grass to get rid of? (Common Couch Grass, or *Agropyron repens,* is a pestilential weed, owing to its creeping rhizomes. — *Penguin Dictionary of British Natural History.*) Couch grass can readily be detected, sending up perky spikes of green from its underworld of rampaging roots and rhizomes. (Rhizome or Rootstock: an underground storage system. *Ibid.*)

So I rang up the council. They told me Plot No. 11 at the Old Northgate Allotments was about to become vacant, and would I like to go and look at it first?

I went, I saw, and was conquered. It was in open country, just beyond the recreation ground. Larks were on the wing. The air was laden with bird-song. And on the plot itself were darling buds of gooseberry and blackcurrant, making a brave show against thickets of dead willow-herb and live docks. I also saw a field-mouse, and a mole on the move; but couch grass was king.

So I went off to the Council for an allotment agreement form, while my wife — still protesting, but with signs of weakening — sent off for a catalogue of gardening tools. One must take advantage of every modern labour-saving device available, she insisted. I argued that gardening tools had not changed fundamentally since Neolithic times. That was talking reactionary nonsense, she said; and the garden-tool catalogues proved her right. For nowadays, it seems, you can buy beautiful cultivators, grubbers, aerators, millers, cleaners, pulverisers, row-markers, sowers, ridgers, and quite a number of multi-purpose tools besides. Above all, it is possible to buy a spade, with levers and grips, that does the digging for you, without your ever having a bend your back.

So I signed the allotment agreement form. I promised to keep Plot No. 11 in good heart.

Well, all that was some weeks ago. Since then we have become, my wife and I, fervent tillers of the soil. We declared war at once on the docks, and infiltrated into the underworld of the couch grass, annihilating it, burning it on great funeral pyres, to the paeans of the larks. While my wife dug away with a modern "ladies' fork," I made my own obeisance to the soil, kneeling upon the good earth itself.

And now the war is almost won, the future bright. Twice a day our plot calls us, weather permitting; early in the morning, when the larks are at their best, rising Icarus-like into the sun; and again early in the afternoon. Immediately the news has finished telling us the worst about the world, we hurry to the open fields and the blessed plot.

Already the onion sets are plumping, the broad beans set with the infant pods, the early potatoes coming into flower, promising economic succour — shining like a good deed in a naughty world. Week by week, if our plans are fulfilled, the rich earth will produce its abundance, continuing through summer and autumn into a winter of purple-sprouting broccoli. And flowers, too, there shall be, to blossom at our behest.

The way things are going — who knows? — we may become self-supporting; living off the land; thriving on spinach-rich vitamins and roughage; and worthy of our earthy name. (Hyde. O.E. Probably holder of a hide of land, sufficient to support a family — *Dictionary of Surnames.*)

4

Inspirations

Miller's Tale

I recently forsook my allotment for a few days to go on pilgrimage to the British Museum Library, there to sit, metaphorically, at the feet of Philip Miller, compiler of *The Gardener's Dictionary,* 1731.

Philip Miller, I would guess — though I stand to be corrected — was the Doctor Johnson of the gardening world. His work is monumental. Merely to lift the great dictionary is to wilt and stagger under its weight. But I found the effort amply repaid. Browsing among the rich prefatorial pages, I gaped at my eighteenth-century namesake listed among the patrons and subscribers; and by way of a 50 per cent bonus, there was also enrolled a Mr Halfhyde, apothecary, of Cambridge. On a modest allotment-holder this bestowed a warm, if unmerited sense of "belonging."

In the preface proper, I read the master's opening words: "Gardening is an exercise excellently adapted to human nature, and the Great Author of All Things, having planted a garden, placed our first parents therein to till and dress it." Then he goes on to extol the virtues of gardening under five heads — Delightfulness, Innocency, Healthfulness, Advantageousness, and Honourableness

"What can be more *delightful* than in the springtime to behold the infant plants putting forth their verdant heads from the bosom of their fostering Mother, the Earth?" he asks, under the first head.

"What indeed?" I reply.

"What employment can be more *innocent?*" he goes on.

"Surely none," I say.

As for *healthfulness,* does not the labour of gardening "prevent the blood and juices from stagnating and growing corrupt?" Does it not "set an edge to the appetite by day, and at night dispose the whole bodily frame into a capacity for the full, enjoyment of those refreshing slumbers, that balmy sleep, whieh generally forsakes the downy couches of the inactive and indolent"?

I agree that it does. For who can deny that among the health-giving recreations of today, gardening is more productive than sport, more tranquil than travel, more genial than demonstrations?

Under the fourth head, Miller reminds us that the *advantages* of gardening are not to be disputed when one sees "what mighty returns repay the favour of the sedulous cultivator." And as for the fifth head — *honourableness* — he points out that Cyrus the Great was a gardener. So was King Solomon. So were Charles II and William IV. Distinction enough! Eminence and to spare!

And so, with my mission accomplished and the words of the master ringing in my ears, I shoulder my fork and make for the allotment — rededicated and renewed — eager to do battle with the couch grass again.

The Testament of a Grand Old Gardener

Our much rained-on allotments have been unpleasantly aqueous and the soil slabby (as they used to say) and clarty (as we still say in these parts). It seemed sensible, therefore, to cultivate the mind instead. A little learning is not necessarily a dangerous thing in these days of exploding technology.

Myself, however, I prefer with advancing age to look back rather than forward: to pick up overlooked or forgotten knowledge of past times. After reading Susan Campbell's attractive publication, *Cottesbrooke — An English Kitchen Garden,* and after viewing television's *Victorian Kitchen Garden* I was inspired to investigate what or who might have brought about this "flowering" of Victorian gardening.

It seems that John Claudius Loudon (b. 1783) and his wife Jane, must be given much of the credit. Loudon seems to have been the inspirer of much of that Victorian gardening enterprise and inventiveness. The son of a Scottish farmer, he came to London at the age of 20 to join the circle of enthusiastic botanists and gardeners around Sir Joseph Banks.

He exhibited landscape paintings at the Royal Academy; farmed; started an agricultural school for young men; advised about the introduction of plane trees to London's smoke-polluted streets and squares; designed, with characteristic restraint and elegance, botanic gardens, park lands, and cemeteries; compiled eight volumes of trees and shrubs, native and imported; produced a 1,000-page *Encyclopaedia of Gardening;* and brought out the first *Gardener's Magazine.*

He became temporarily rich, married the charming non-gardening novelist, Jane Webb; went to live in Porchester Terrace in semi-rural Bayswater; and travelled extensively, looking at agricultural and gardening innovations of good taste. He went to Moscow over battlefields just vacated by the retreating Napoleon, and met British gardeners surprisingly employed by Russians. Later he went through France and Italy, noticing such details as the use by gardeners in Monza of square plant pots to save greenhouse space.

In Venice he secured a specimen aquatic plant, then unknown in England, named after the Italian botanist A. Vallesneri. The flowers of *Vallisneria spiralis,* had the curious habit of rising to the water surface for fertilisation, then spiralling back below. He carried his specimen in a can, on muleback through the Simplon Pass to Paris where he put it on his bedroom window ledge. Next morning, alas, it was gone, consumed by voracious sparrows. In this and other ways he was beaten, but his dedication and drive continued undiminished.

It was while working on his *Arboretum et Fruticetum Britannicum* that he is said to have sought permission to inspect the Duke of Wellington's famous beeches. But a hurried reading of his letter led to the Bishop of London not Loudon receiving a parcel containing the duke's breeches, as worn at Waterloo. Loudon never overlooks the plotholders and cottage gardeners, saying it is a sin to put away tools uncleaned; not carry a garden knife; drop a hoe with blade uppermost; or stride across crop rows; and garden in a hurry. And always know your plant's names.

He advocated growing elders in cottage gardens for their valuable flowers and berries, a state we should return to now that hedgerow elderberries are non-existent or tainted. He suggested raising them at no cost from whips or cuttings, and training them three to five feet high. Indeed there were elderberry orchards in Kent: bark, leaves, flowers, and berries all had their uses.

Loudon describes the blackcurrant as a humble shrub found in alder swamps, wet hedges, and sometimes in woods. The name gooseberry, he suggests, was a corruption of gorseberry because it resembled that prickly bush. And he wrote a book on growing pineapples.

The tireless energy and drive of John Claudius Loudon — he was said not to sit down or to eat between 7am and 8pm — resulted, however, in his becoming disabled. When surgeons arrived at his home to amputate his right arm, they found him in his garden to which, he said, he intended to return immediately after the operation. He died while dictating to Jane his last book, *Self-instruction to Young Gardeners.* She completed it, reissued other of his works, and wrote books of her own.

No full biography of Loudon has appeared perhaps it is too colossal a task but Geoffrey Taylor has praised him in his book, *Some Nineteenth Century Gardens.*

Under the Gooseberry Bush

After a somewhat difficult spring, early summer became merry and marvellous on our burgeoning allotments, not only for plotholders but also for the new generation of piratical young rabbits. They are cursed by most, tolerated by a live-and-let-live few, and by one of our number — who has an excellent rapport with animals — taken home to his family for adoption, and housed with a fostering mother rabbit. One man in the Pennines, I read, keeps his raiding rabbits at bay with a pet weasel.

The larks and yellow hammers, however, are nowadays by no means as merry or as many as I remember them to have been ten years ago, when I used to rise at dawn and go to the allotments to share their early summer joy. The birds were perhaps even merrier in John Loudon's day, when he published his weighty *Encyclopaedia of Gardening*. Chemicals were not then in fashion. Muck was in vogue. Soot and soft soap were gardeners' standbys. Straw was used to protect against frost and strong sun. Brushwood twigs and branches kept predators off seed rows and young crops. In fact things were done pretty much as cottage gardeners still do them today.

Loudon's massive book, dictated to his devoted wife and amanuensis, Jane Loudon, is eminently quotable: "The love of gardens is the only passion which augments with age," or again, "A poor man will eat better that has a garden of his own than a rich man that has none." That is what my plot neighbour, Nelson, and myself have been telling each other for years. It would be a good enough motto for any allotment society to adopt.

The advice that Loudon gives may be old fashioned but it is none the worse for that, and it tallies remarkably with the advice that Nelson likes to give me — like the use of soot on onion beds or to annoy pests, or the stalking and trapping of cutworms at the base of young cabbage plants, or the inclusion of prickly furze pieces in pea drills to deter mice, or the hand picking of defoliating caterpillars in due season.

In John Loudon's day, cottage gardeners had little alternative but to save seeds from their own crops. He advised to take seed always from the healthiest plants. This process of selection, we may suppose, produced the interesting and reliable varieties that L.D. Hills of the Henry Doubleday Research Association wants to save in his vegetable sanctuaries. He names as worthy of saving, the onions Up-to-date and Rousham Park Hero, the first resistant to downy mildew, the second to white rot; the Pot Leek of the Durham miners; the broccoli Knight's Protecting for it hardiness in winter; the cabbage Velocity with a growing season of 14 weeks; the cabbage Stockley's Giant Red, which he describes as "too good for picking"; a tasty small turnip, November Green Top; a carrot, Altrincham, which grows up to twenty inches long; a greenhouse tomato, Market King, and an outdoor tomato, Davington Epicure, whose taste and thin skins, Mr Hill says, are to be recommended.

On the soft fruits, Loudon's *Encyclopaedia* is always interesting. In his time elderberry trees were grown in cottage gardens for their fruit. He advocated raising them from cuttings and training them as standards, three to five feet high, allowing the tops to branch out. The raspberry, he says, was "grateful to most palates." It liked a light rich loam, continued in perfection five or six years, but needed then to be replaced with good stock.

The blackcurrant he described as a humble shrub, to be found in Britain in alder swamps, in wet hedges, on the banks of rivers, and sometimes in woods. In Russia it was forced in pots for the fragrance of the leaves. There were at that time no varieties.

The gooseberry (a corruption, he supposed, of gorseberry because it resembled a prickly gorse bush) had more than 300 varieties. In Lancashire and Cheshire almost every cottage garden had its gooseberry bushes, and hopes of prizes at what were called gooseberry prize meetings. These events were recorded in an annual publication, *The Manchester Gooseberry Book*. Loudon examined the *Gooseberry Book* for 1819 which reported no fewer than 136 meetings. The largest berry that year was the Top-Sawyer Seedling, a red fruit weighing 26 pennyweights, 17 grams. There were on exhibition 46 red, 33 yellow, 47 green, and 41 white sorts; and 14 new named seedlings, stated as "going out" — that is, about to be sold to propagators.

The Lancashire gooseberry connoisseur sowed seeds of choice varieties in pots of rich light soil and planted them out after a year to be cultivated and trained for a year or two. The best of these young bushes were then given a favoured treatment — a rich soil, watering, shading and thinning of the fruit to get the largest specimens. Not only were they watered at the root and over the top, but the exhibitor placed a small saucer of water immediately under each gooseberry, only three or four being left on the bush; this process was called suckling.

Not being a Lancastrian, I don't know if the tradition is continued or improved on, but I do know of a North Yorkshireman who provides his bushes with umbrellas — against too much sun or thunder shower, one supposes. We are not gooseberry fanciers on our enclave, but we have welcomed a good crop to give us a reasonable vintage of champagne-type green gooseberry wine.

Place for Women

The influence of women on gardening seems always to have been of a committed and pioneering nature. It was the "women weeders" of Tudor times who kept the stately gardens trim. Only in more recent times have Western women gone agoraphobically indoors, to drudgery, housewifery, career jobs, coffee mornings, and afternoon bridge.

Though many housewives do undertake and enjoy home gardening, statistics show that in the realm of allotmenteering only three out of every hundred plot-holders are women. Worse, it appears that those wives who give their plot-holding husbands a helping hand are but a small minority.

Professor Thorpe's 1969 *Allotments Report* explains this by stating that women "tend to be more fastidious than men about the conditions under which they will engage in their hobbies," and goes on to suggest that "the lack of decent facilities, and absence of any strong social activity and the general air of dereliction on many allotment sites probably act as considerable deterrents."

There are, of course, less gallant explanations: witness the old North-country saying — "Two things ye mun keep out o' t' garden: a wumman and a scratting' hen."

Professor Thorpe, however, firmly believes that women will be the salvation of the allotment precisely because they are so much better organisers than men — besides being more sociable. To give but one example, there is a large and prosperous private allotment site in Birmingham whose organising secretary, Mrs M. Alton, also finds time to work her own charmingly appointed sun-catching little plot.

Birmingham, surprisingly to an outsider, has over twelve thousand allotments. Perhaps its citizens are inspired by the example of that admirable Birmingham-born lady gardener of early Victorian times, Jane Loudon.

Wife of the famous John *Encyclopaedia of Gardening* Loudon, she patiently picked up her gardening lore from him and became in her own right the first professional lady-gardener in the country. She wrote books to lure Victorian ladies out of their stuffy drawing-rooms and persuade them to take up the spade in their garden-gloved hands. She herself designed the gardening gloves.

I certainly recommend the biography of this model lady-gardener, *Lady with Green Fingers,* by Bea Howe.

Women's Realm

One of the good things about allotments is the fellow-feeling that can emerge alongside respect for the loner's wish to communicate only with his own drops. For me, the community spirit was highlighted during two months of relative inactivity away from my plot, fearing all the while that it would revert to the riotous freedom of nature.

I need not have worried. Arnold, whose own plot is a picture, found time to bring mine up to scratch. Ken banked up my potatoes and sowed peas. Sheila mowed my grass paths, and with her husband Keith, planted my onion sets.

Sheila and Keith, retired academics, have a near perfect plot of high quality crops — minus brassicas, to avoid the club root scourge. They have a love of gardening in our enclave of rural tranquility situated sufficiently far from all madding crowds and Chelsea.

It is good to see parents with children and sometimes grandparents on plots. Many old-timers can recall with nostalgia the allotments of their own parents.

Women are generally more careful and conscientious in a garden than men, showing perhaps more imagination and patience, enjoying the scented fresh air and open sky especially in May and June. I imagine it was always so from neolithic and medieval times to the women weeders of Elizabethan days who were no slaves, the more refined Victorian lady gardeners, and the trained experts of our own day.

Jane and John Loudon are among the most famous garden partnerships. John Claudius Loudon, born in 1783, perhaps the greatest of early 19th century gardeners, was a workaholic, on his feet all day out of doors, and until late at night indoors, dictating, with Jane, his wife and amanuensis, taking down every word of his *Gardeners'*

Encyclopaedia and of the profitable issues of his *Gardener's Magazine.*

Their marriage may be considered romantic. Jane, a young novelist, had written a fantasy of the future, including a steam plough. (One was manufactured a few years later.) John reviewed the book, contrived to meet the author, found her to be an attractive young lady, married her (dictating his work in hand while dressing for the wedding), and to all appearances they lived a life of devotion, of hard work and extensive travel.

They toured this country and post-Napoleonic Europe. At Alton Towers they found bridges over dry land, pools in impossible places, and women tirelessly "weeding, sweeping, picking up dead leaves and insects, cutting decayed flowers, and tying up straggling shoots" for their opulent employer. John Claudius Loudon died still on his feet, dictating his latest book. Jane caught him in her arms, and his head fell on her shoulder. She lived on for 15 years to write her own gardening books and to renew some of her husband's. Geoffrey Taylor tells the story in his book (*Some 19th Century Gardeners* — Skeffington, 1957) which was favourably reviewed by Harold Nicholson, husband of Sissinghurst's Vita Sackville-West — another gardening partnership.

One wonders what Jane and John, or Harold and Vita, would have made of this year's Chelsea Show — some reservations, one imagines. William "Back to Nature" Robinson's reaction, you could guess, would have been outright disapproval for artificiality and too much precision, over-stringing, flashiness, and an excess of design. However, he would have approved — I hope — of John Chambers's quiet yet controlled wild flower garden and of Leyhill Open Prison's productive Edible garden radiant with ornamental cabbages and (to quote Tom Bussman) with its "witty use of Dartmoor stone, lots of thyme, but naturally no grass."

Living Canvas by Bumps

A Chinese proverb has it that if you want to be happy for a week, get married; for a month, kill a pig; for a lifetime, plant a garden.

Though not piggishly chauvinistic enough to echo the first pronouncement, I heartily endorse the last. And now that I am inclined to hear time's wingéd chariot hovering near, and see deserts of vast eternity not too far ahead, I am determined to make the most of my remaining years both in my secluded garden and on my open-space allotment.

Thanks to a very favourable, sometimes glorious, October, my 10-rod plot is now reasonably ship-shape — the grass paths trimmed for their winter sleep; the rubbish cleared; the gooseberry and currant bushes pruned; weeds cleared from overwintering onions, brassicas, and Swiss chard; and some digging done.

We oldies can find digging soothing and satisfying, even enjoyable — particularly if we take it in small doses and choose good weather and soil conditions. We need to be well clad, of course, well shod, and equipped with spades of good balance to suit our size. Thus occupied on this repetitive job, the mind is free to wander and daydream.

The other day, for instance, it was the portrait of Miss Jekyll, the lady gardener, that flashed before my inner eye. She helped with the spadework in the early days of the Wisley garden, I had learned. And then it was the charming picture of her Gardening Boots that I saw. That picture I surmised, would look well if paired with Van Gogh's Chair.

Gertrude Jekyll (1843–1932) — G.J. for short and called Bumps by her friends — was fat, friendly and fearless.

Born of gentlefolk, she lived near Godalming in west Surrey. As a child she roamed freely along the country lanes, knew the wild flowers by name and smell and the birds in dialect. The green woodpecker was Yaffles, the wren Puggy, and the dragonflies skimming the pond Adder Spears.

She mixed with the villagers, admired their cottage gardens, learned their crafts, and made some of her own gardening tools at the blacksmith's forge. And she appears to have been completely classless. For instance, she helped by letter a Lancashire mill lad seeking advice on the use of his few square feet of soil (it seems to have been an attic window box in Rochdale) and followed this up with a postal package of plants, bulbs, and pebbles to complete his project.

Her ambition to be a painter was thwarted by acute shortness of sight which made her turn to gardening, "making pictures with living plants" to use her own words; and she became famous for the gardens she created and the books she wrote.

Eminent Victorians and gardeners who visited her by now famous Munstead Wood home found her wearing two pairs of spectacles. Far from moping about her painful and progressive myopia, she declared it to be an advantage because, having to peer so closely, she could detect objects that the well-sighted passed without noticing.

And her other senses were accentuated. She could hear a hedgehog moving "noiselessly" in the undergrowth, distinguish trees by the rustle of their leaves in the wind and the feel of their bark, and know the nearness of flowers by their scents. Lupins for her had a peppery smell, bracken a smell of the sea.

Knowing this, I am stirred to re-educate my own neglected senses by moving about the allotment with my eyes almost closed when no-one is looking (Miss Jekyll used to jump five-bar gates when no-one was looking.) I can then learn by its tic-tic that the robin is my feet, judge by smell that I have trodden on thyme or bumped into a rosemary bush, and tell by touch that the leaf in my hand is comfrey and not common dock.

Miss Jekyll's books are pleasantly readable and as uncluttered as their titles — *Home and Garden; Wood and Garden; Children and Gardens; Old West Surrey* . . . this last with 300 photographs to record early Victorian life in those parts.

Her articles too, written for magazines and journals, are always readable and informative. Some of these were reprinted in book form after her death — *A Gardener's Testament,* published by *Country Life* and Scribner, New York, in 1937.

Her books are still available in reference and some lending libraries, and there is a more recent biography, *Miss Jekyll — Portrait of a Great Gardener,* by Bessy Massingham, David and Charles, 1966.

The later years of her long and successful life were troubled, alas, by an excess of curious and unannounced visitors in addition to the genuine and eminent gardeners whom she welcomed. "Many Americans, Germans and journalists," she noted sadly. It would not be surprising if Japanese tourists now go in search of gardens she created, or of the grave into which her coffin was gently lowered by gardeners in 1932.

Prickly Producer

Is it reasonable to suppose that some of the unconverted will have made a New Year resolution to join the band of organic gardeners, or at least to go part way? If so, they might like a few pointers to where to look for elucidation and help.

For me, organic gardening is as practised by my father in the early years of this century, and by my grandfather before him. They dug and double dug. Organic manures were easily available — farmyard, stable, poultry.

There was soot in plenty, wood ash, and a ready supply of soft soap; gorse bushes provided prickles to plant with the peas against thieving mice, and briar stumps were plunged into mole runs to annoy and deter those little beasts. Chemical sprays — to their knowledge — were neither needed nor available, artificial fertilisers largely unknown. But there was muck aplenty.

It was exactly 20 years ago that I first heard of Lawrence D. Hills, that passionate advocate of organic gardening. His death will, for many, leave a gap. His vivid and stimulating writings will be missed. He founded the Henry Doubleday Research Association (HDRA) in 1954, as a friendly, environment-conscious body.

HDRA is a group of "green", horticulturally experimenting amateurs and professionals which began in a small way but has proliferated to international membership and recognition. Henry Doubleday was a 19th century Quaker smallholder in Coggeshall, Essex, of the same family as the American Doubleday publishers.

As a member of the Royal Agricultural Society of England (RASE) and an avid reader of its journal, Doubleday was driven to action by an article entitled *On The Composition And Nutritive Value Of The Prickly Comfrey,* and envisaged the time when this quick-growing, deeprooted, protein-rich, potash-producing plant might one day free the world of famine. Accordingly, he acquired some Russian comfrey plants to grow in Coggeshall.

Inspired by Doubleday's example, 50 years after his death, Lawrence D. Hills acquired a smallholding at Bocking, near Braintree, where he planted comfrey to study the types and crosses of the plant. He observed the variations of flower colour, leaf shape, and plant size, and labelled the types with Bocking numbers.

Number B14 is considered best for gardeners. I have grown a controlled crop on my allotment for years, using it as a — I hope — potash-laden green manure which turns black when cut. You can plant root offsets in any month except December and January, two inches deep and two feet apart, and you cut it regularly to stop it flowering. The roots apparently go down as far as 10 feet to draw up nutrients that, normally, only trees can reach. So aggressively does it spread that gardeners have been known to ask how to get rid of it. You cut it off at the root and apply a little sodium chlorate weed killer.

To bring the HDRA story up to date: it expanded, and moved, in 1985, to Coventry where, as the National Centre for Organic Gardening at Ryton-on-Dunsmore, it is now the well established home of the HDRA and rapidly developing under the leadership of Alan Gear and its council members.

It is concerned with matters other than the magic comfrey. Horticultural and ecological fears, affairs, and developments are aired in its quarterly magazine. Of particular interest to an organic beginner is the series of 8-16 page pull-outs entitled *Step By Step Organic Gardening*.

Going Back to Our Roots

During the allotment off-season, I find time to read about gardeners of the past. William Robinson (1838–1935) is one such.

Irish by birth, he was a back-to-nature gardener of Victorian times and beyond, aggressively opposed to the formal gardening of his day. He makes me feel less guilty about my overgrown and wildish home garden.

From a poor garden boy in Ireland, William Robinson lived to become the squire of Gravetye Manor, an Elizabethan mansion set in acres of wild land in West Hoathly, Sussex.

Little is known of the young Robinson's early life in Ireland, though his date of birth suggests that he grew up during those tragic years of potato famine and starvation which could well have affected his future character and combative temperament.

By the age of 21, he had become foreman of his employer's extensive glasshouses and conservatories, which were filled with tender and tropical plants.

It was then that he committed his act of vandalism, opening all the doors and windows on a frosty winter's night, raking out the stoves, and leaving for Dublin, to cross without delay to London. His criminal act behind him, he seems never to have looked back. His reverend employer could perhaps forgive.

The Royal Botanical Society's Garden in Regent's Park took him on at 9s. a week to look after herbaceous plant and a garden of English wild flowers.

This was clearly to his liking. He roamed outlying woodlands, meadows and hillsides searching for suitable plants — not then a culpable activity. He travelled in France, hated Versailles, visited North Africa and its natural rock gardens, and went to North America during the colourful autumn.

He came to own and edit garden weeklies and journals, wrote many books including the *Wild Garden* and *The English Flower Garden* — the 1000-page eleventh edition (1909) of which I found in a local library.

His entrepreneurial prowess brought him wealth. He bought up London property, met celebrities such as Ruskin and Darwin, struck up a surprisingly strong friendship with that amiable lady gardener Gertrude Jekyll, and helped her with her famous Munstead Garden.

He bought and lived for half a century in Gravetye Manor where, at the age of 72, becoming paralysed in his legs, he was obliged to supervise his 200-acre estate from a motorised wheelchair. When he died at 97, he left his wildish estate to a more neglectful public.

Throughout his life, Robinson had vigorously advocated the growing of hardy plants in places where they could fend for themselves.

The advantages of a wild garden, he said, are that many hardy flowers both thrive better and look better in rough places; that their decaying and dying is better concealed; and that you can grow more flowers than is possible in a trim garden. The informality of a cottage garden was always his ideal.

He resisted all artificiality — bedding out, parterres, garden ornaments, topiary, flower shows, exhibitions of "improved plants," glasshouses (he demolished the lot at Gravetye) and, with Ruskin, the excessive used of Latin botanical names. Me too.

His contemporaries variously described him as plain-spoken, controversial, peevish, and eccentric. He though the best way to look at a landscape was to turn round, bend down with feet astride, and look between your legs. I seem to remember G.K. Chesterton giving the same advice.

With hindsight, we can call William Robinson a character. With foresight, we can see the labour-saving advantages of his style of gardening. With reservations, I can go along with him.

Freedom to Potter

With spring in the air, it is good for a confessed oldie to be facing another allotment year. I should be at a loss without a garden or allotment to walk or work in at will.

In an ideal society, I suppose, everyone who wanted a suitable plot to cultivate would find one conveniently available. Also, schools, homes for the elderly and hospitals would give high priority to surrounding grounds and gardens. Prisons, too. If I were detained, I would hope to be in an open prison and able to supply my fellow inmates with fresh vegetables.

Leigh Hunt began a two-year stretch in February, 1813 for libelling the Prince Regent, and found the prison garden in Horsemonger's Lane, off Newington Causeway — "the Surrey prison" — a great boon. He was permitted to continue editing his reformist periodical, the *Examiner,* but first brightened up his "Home and Garden" prison environment.

Being of uncertain health, he was given a room in the infirmary wing which he decorated with blue sky and fleecy clouds painted on the ceiling. The walls he papered with a rose and trellis design. This done, he could have his family reside with him and his literary friends visit him — Shelley, Keats, Byron, Hazlitt, Charles Lamb...

Outside his room was a small yard into which — while the year was yet young — he had loads of good soil dumped for flower growing and, in summer, Scarlet Runners on trellis. And since a door opened from this yard into the prison garden itself and to springtime cherry blossom, he could walk or work there, and play with his children.

At liberty on my own allotment, I have been annihilating the infant weeds since January, using a long-handled dutch hoe and working only from the paths. Plot holders adopting the narrow bed system have the advantage here. Nowadays, much mulching is advocated to keep down weeds but the perennial ones are best dug up, root and rhizome, to be burned on small weed-built funeral pyres, of couch grass, ground elder, bindweed, docks, and creeping thistles. As a last resort, there are the chemical weedkillers.

In past years, my plot companion Nelson would never have allowed these more modern and less honourable methods to supplant hoeing and hand weeding of crops. Now alas, at 86, and recently sadly widowed, he no longer has the urge to attack and conquer those "unwanted plants" and "plants in the wrong place" in pursuit of the pristine plot.

Rusticated to a Fertile Plot

Sydney Smith, the broadminded cleric and witty letter writer who in the early 1800s was rusticated to the village glebe of Foston near York, was obliged to farm for a living on the fringe of the Castle Howard estate. Some of his fertile acres he turned into plots — 16 to the acre — for the villagers. Dutch gardens, he called them. I have thought of those early allotments while working on my own rural plot and recalled serene spring days of long ago when I lived in my youth on Monument Farm close by Foston.

Sydney Smith told of the pleasure it gave him to see his parishioners out on their plots in the early morning sunshine. Then — at 6am — he hailed his farmworkers to his own employ through a large speaking trumpet kept inside the rectory door.

This clubbable city man turned farmer was idolised by his servants and cheerfully admitted that he also performed the duties of schoolmaster, doctor, magistrate and dietician to his flock. Himself something of a gourmet, he was an expert with salads.

At first, on bad advice, he bought four oxen and named them Tug, Lug, Haul, and Crawl, but soon changed these for gentle cart horses, possibly named Bonny, Beauty and Blossom as ours were on the nearby farm. And believing, as he said, in cheap luxuries, even for animals, he built for them a scratching pole, stretching between a low and a high post, to accommodate animals of all sizes from lamb to horse. This ebullient and admirable man was a friend of the needy peacher but critic of "the shooting parsons of Malton".

The plot holders of today perhaps find such beneficence thinner on the ground, but at least they don't lack for good gardening advice from the media and from horticultural associations and organisations.

Take NIAB — the National Institute of Agricultural Botany. NIAB has a revised booklet, *Vegetable Varieties For Gardeners,* now available as a Wisley handbook. This gives information about the many varieties currently available in catalogues and can help a gardener choose the best variety for a particular season or situation, and indeed much else.

The trials look for crops with higher yields, improved performance, greater disease resistance and better quality and flavour.

There are also individual vegetable leaflets mainly for the commercial grower but of interest to the enterprising allotmenteer; and a booklet, *Vegetable Varieties For The Organic Grower,* which considers such additional aspects as the relative vigour of varieties with less access to nitrogen, the ability to develop a good root system, or to grow a leafy canopy to smother weeds.

How to Hatch a Plot

Cold April north-easters and worsening weather disrupted for a while the noiseless tenor of our allotment way. Nevertheless, the rhubarb — which can withstand hail, frost, and snow — glows with good health. Meanwhile the spring cabbages, benefiting from earlier as well as more recent mildness, are hearting nicely and becoming individually shapely.

The Royal Horticultural Society, with the National Vegetable Society, held a one-day seminar for amateur vegetable enthusiasts in the assembly hall of the Harrogate Royal Baths. It attracted about one hundred gardeners to a programme of useful talks with the slogan: "If it's not fit to eat, it's not fit to show." This, however, did not deter experts from letting us into the secrets of growing pot leeks and producing giant celery by dint of dedication.

The talk on protective cropping revealed dangers — scorching, for instance — as well as the advantages of using polythene. How to recycle polythene was seen as a problem in need of attention.

The curator of Harrogate Harlow Car Gardens told how their vegetable trials concentrated on finding varieties most suitable to northern conditions. He gave good reasons for amateur vegetable growers to visit these beautiful and developing Northern Horticultural Society gardens to which members of the RHS can gain free admission. A useful handout list — *Disorders, Diseases and Pests of Vegetables* — compiled by Wisley experts, was served to us. Though reluctant myself to digest such a discomfortingly long list of ills that vegetables are heir to, I shall certainly keep it handy for reference.

I shall therefore know, for, instance, that orange-yellow bands between the veins of tomato leaves denote magnesium deficiency and a need for Epsom Salts; or that the browning of curds on my cauliflowers indicates a boron deficiency, preventable by an application of borax, one ounce to 20 sq yd, applied well bulked with light sand.

Back on the plot, and daunted by so many direful vegetable afflictions, I have decided to concentrate this season on my herb and flower section, occupying one-third of the plot. Already I have flowers being raised in pots to be put out as soon as I feel confident that they can withstand the rigours of allotment life. Unwin's sweet peas are already in position and climbing their tall canes.

Adding to my herb section, I have sown small patches of Florence fennel, lemon balm, coriander, dill, and chervil, first stirring some seed compost into the surface soil for encouragement.

While sowing these herb seeds, I muse — as I am wont to do — on the historical herbalists, Culpeper and Gerard. Those two gentlemen have long been only names to me, an unsatisfactory state of affairs for any self-respecting allotmenteer. I therefore took down my much-neglected compact edition of the *National Dictionary of Biography* with its accompanying magnifying glass and acquired, with considerable eye strain, a little dangerous knowledge about them.

Nicholas Culpeper, I learn, lived in those days of civil strife and disturbed gardening when cavalier Cavaliers no doubt rode roughshod over many a garden plot while chasing Roundheads. Born in London, educated at Cambridge, he studied Latin, Greek, and the old medical writers. He translated foreign herbal works and compiled his own.

Culpeper was an astrologer-physician, a profession of which I had been unaware. He set up his practice in Spitalfields, married, had seven children, lived in straitened circumstances, but nevertheless gave free advice to the poor.

He fought for Cromwell, was wounded in the chest, and died at the age of 38. Whether this was due to the chest wound or to his own herbal remedies is a matter for speculation. His *English Physician Enlarged With 360 Medicines Made of English Herbs* was published the year before he died. I am indebted to my daughter for sending me a copy of Foulsham's *Culpeper's Complete Herbal.*

John Gerard was born half-a-century earlier and may be said to have been a Royalist since he was gardener to James I and superintendent of Lord Burghley's gardens in the Strand and at Theobalds in Hertfordshire. His own excellent garden was in Holborn.

Gerard was born in Cheshire and became a skilled herbalist. His handsome *Herbal,* dedicated to Lord Burghley, was priced 25s 6d when it was published. A recent edition (Dover), my daughter informs me, costs £60. (She has not sent me a copy.)

Gerard had suffered from ague, I learn, for which Culpeper could have offered him a choice of 19 herbal cures, including Agrimony and Bilberries (under the dominion of Jupiter), Black Hellebore (Saturn), Hops, and the Blessed Thistle (Mars).

How far astrology affects our allotments is a matter for conjecture. Plotters do come and go. Eric, our young enthusiast and model gardener, has had to give up his patch owing to pressure of work, alas.

But Andrew, a Norfolk giant and excellent gardener who left us years ago to return to his native King's Lynn, has reappeared like a ghost to inhabit another plot and be faced by a mystery. He has found spread out in front of his recently broken-into shed, the head, abdomen, and one leg of a rat. Is this, he wonders, a ritual curse laid by a human hand, or the left-overs of a predator's meal?

Life on the allotments is never dull; and the birds sing merrily in May.

Holding
Your Ground

Gardening for Leisure

"Mother Nature usually compensates," my market gardening neighbour told me over the allotment hedge last spring. He was standing, I remember, among his waterlogged and wasted spring cabbages; and it seemed to me, at the time, an expression of blind faith. But events proved him right.

As it in answer to that dread rumour, one of the vacant and neglected plots came under new tenancy. A mixed foursome took it on. They were people in their prime; they would not have looked out of place in the company of Miss Jean Brodie. Each evening they arrived by carload with all appropriate tools and worked till the sunset sky turned to pale parsnip with streaks of broccoli blue.

This refreshing enterprise sprang up within 50 yards of our plot, so that I was able to observe it with a discreet, unprying eye. But it was not until the publication of Professor Harry Thorpe's *Allotments Report* in the autumn that I saw these newcomers in a clear and wholly admirable light. They had come to us as Leisure Gardeners of the New Age — inspired innovators, visionary revolutionaries. It was almost as if they had been sent by Professor Thorpe himself.

Because Professor Thorpe and his committee have important things to tell us allotment-holders — things which we must heed. For instance, we must get rid without delay of the zinc baths and old bedsteads, along with the outdated image of the allotment as a "charitable dole of land" for the labouring poor. The new Leisure Gardens must prove worthy of the many prospective tenants who could derive joy and benefit from them — the flat dwellers and office workers who need the feel of the earth under their feet and the tang of fresh air in their nostrils; the architects, doctors, and teachers in need of recreation; the ladies and the retired of both sexes.

Gardening, it must be insisted, is as much a recreation as, say, golf. Public golf courses have their car parks and club houses; why should not allotted leisure gardens have these amenities too? Let us hope they are on their way; and if a little militancy will get them moving — then so be it. Allotmenteers unite! With Professor Harry Thorpe and Nature behind us, who is to say us nay?

The Amateurs and the Clod Bashers

All available allotments on our site are under the spade this year; and I am told there is a waiting list. This is a welcome change. Last year, something like half the plots were wild prairies by mid-summer. Then came the rumour that we were to be dispossessed and the land given over to market-gardening, which brought us smartly up to attention.

As a result we are now giving more time and care to our cultivated enclave; though we still have a rose-grower who takes a plot for two years, buds and blooms his roses, reaps his bonanza and then moves on, leaving the next man to clear the docks and thistles and put some goodness back into the soil. It takes all sorts...

The newer tenants on our site appear to be a cross-section of the community, including on the one hand gardening amateurs from the professional classes and on the other the down-to-earth "clod-bashers" whose rural forebears lived off the land until they were dispossessed of it by those despicable "enclosures" that drove people off the land into the towns, or on to the parish poor relief. It was then that the allotment was born (by the landed benefactor out of charity) on a pauper's bed of dole.

Different parts of the country thought up different rules. In some places regular church attendance was a condition of tenancy; and it was just too bad if the sabbath turned out to be an ideal day for planting potatoes. Other allotmenteers were forbidden to work their plots between the hours of 6am and 6pm — during which time, of course all their energy and labour was due to the landowner who hired them.

Some of the tiny, one-storey cottages of our own pauper's gardens (mercifully re-named "New Village") survive to this day. They are photogenic, especially the one with a large and splendidly blooming magnolia tree at its door.

Since 1919 allotments have been open to all comers, irrespective of status or occupation. But the stigma of "charity" remains, as stigmas are wont to do. "Leisure Gardens," it was suggested, would promote a new image; but is it acceptable to the local councils, some of whom still equate leisure with indolence?

Local councils have been known to appoint allotment inspectors to look out for shirkers. Our own council, having removed the broken glass and rusty bottomless buckets from our site, has issued a circular letter reminding us of the new allotment competition, in which every plot is to be judged for cultivation, lay-out, neatness and variety.

There is no opting out: we are all in it, willy-nilly. In the old days of *laissez faire* you could pay your shilling and enter the competition, or you could stand idly by with a smug smile on your face, as the unambitious and those tolerant of bedsteads lying about, usually did. But things are to be different this year. We don't have to pay a shilling but we do have to compete.

The old soldiers among us will be quick to detect traces of regimental discipline; the octogenarian old-timers will be voluble in defending precedent, and the influx of middle-class amateurs will no doubt be vigilant against any resurgence of bumbledom. Meanwhile the crops grow apace and look good, taking our minds off thoughts and actions usually associated with long hot summers, and promoting, rather, a sense of well-fed euphoria.

Altruistic Toil

Allotment gardening is now officially recognised as a recreation; indeed, plot-holding representatives are now co-opted on Recreational Services Committees. Not all councillors, however, can get away from the notion that the provision of allotments is a kind of old-fashioned charity, to be administered grudgingly. Nevertheless, good relations can usually be maintained where plot-holders cooperate and keep their plots under control.

During the summer months, for instance, the tireless plot-holder must face up to the arch-enemy – weed infestation – with stout heart and robust resolution. But to enjoy gardening above all other interests – dotes on it, and lavish time on it – then the plot-holder can give to a standard ten-rod plot the care it demands in return for worthy vegetables, flowers and fruit. Nothing less will suffice.

On our enclave, with a few notable exceptions, it is the clubbable pensioners who can put in enough time and single-minded concentration to maintain their plots to a standard of excellence. One of our number chivalrously volunteers, in deserving cases, to rescue other plots in distress rather than see them conquered by couch grass and summer weeds. His vigour and accomplishments are phenomenal.

Practically every day his back is bent to his good works, and is only straightened to point out to a passer-by the thistle-down drifting on the breeze to proliferate its species on other plots. "Some people," he opines, "don't deserve to have plots. They think all they have to do is to plant up in spring and then wait till the crops are ready." He shakes his head ruefully, and returns to his altruistic toil. (Dilettante gardeners and starry-eyed applicants for plots, please note.)

The allotment superintendent of a near-by city tells me his council gives 14 days' notice to a tenant of a neglected plot, together with a bill for the cost of bringing it back into cultivation. To avoid having to pay this, the tenant must convincingly plead extenuating circumstances in good time. Discipline, indeed!

The late Professor Thorpe of the 1969 *Allotments Report* was for discipline too. He sought to change our allotment eyesores into respectable peaceful and park-like places for keen and self-disciplined gardeners to enjoy to the full their chosen recreation.

He wanted to abolish the very name "allotment." Nor would he accept "recreational garden" as a substitute, since the mischievous, he thought, would quickly have contracted it to a diminutive and homonymous (w)rec(k). So "leisure garden" it had to be — an unhappy choice, perhaps, and one which I cannot bring myself to use.

But Professor Harry Thorpe made his mark on the allotment scene; and courageously delayed his entry into hospital until he had given his welcoming address to recreational gardeners from abroad at the international congress held in Birmingham last September. Now it is left for his disciples to carry on his work on behalf of future recreational gardeners.

I made a brief visit to the National Conference of Leisure Gardeners, and met Professor Thorpe colleague from the Birmingham University Allotment Research Unit, Mrs Elizabeth Galloway. Mrs Galloway assured me that plot-holders of the new-look Birmingham Leisure Gardens are happy, and indeed proud of their landscaped environment and their not-always-rectangular plots. Her recent publication *Design for Leisure Gardening* outlines imaginative possibilities and their practical application.

Tyneside's Chief Recreation and Amenities Officer got his listeners into a jolly mood before dropping the information that his authority had decided to give 28 days' notice to raise rents instead of the statutory 12 months; whereupon, with a growing roar, he was pounced on.

A delegate from Hampshire informed him that a council in her own area, on being challenged, had had to retract from a similar bold move. However, in return for the retraction the thousand plot-holders of the Gosport Allotments Association have agreed to take on the responsibility of administering their own sites.

Tom Hume, allotments consultant of the London Association of Recreational Gardeners, tells of Continental gardening associations who pool their own varied skills to do construction and maintenance work for which the authorities provide the materials. It is this kind of thing which can keep the rents down, the plot-holders happy and the council landlords placated.

Allotments in Demand

I received a letter from a correspondent in Hampstead, most of which I reproduce (with her permission) below:

I am without a garden here for the first time in my life. The lovely rambling front garden was covered in asphalt a month after we signed a five-year lease. Trees, flowers — everything ripped out and thrown away. There are three cars there now . . .

I went to the town hall to sign on for an allotment. I am number seventeen on the waiting list (number one has been waiting for five years). I wrote to the railways having noticed several abandoned allotments near the lines. 'Sorry — you have to be a railway employee.' I used to be and my father worked on the railway for forty years, but that was no help. I contacted the Citizens' Advice Bureau, who gave me the addresses of various local gardening/horticultural societies. I wrote to these; they didn't reply.

There are so many gardens in and around Hampstead that are totally neglected that I eventually plucked up courage and knocked on a door, asking the person who opened it if I could care for his garden. 'We don't have the money for that sort of rubbish' was the reply. When I said I'd do it for nothing he replied 'Yes — and I'm the Duke of Edinburgh,' and banged the door. I could see the funny side of this encounter, but it did sap the last little dregs of courage I had, so my next step was to put an ad. in a newsagent's window: 'I will care for your neglected garden. Grow vegetables, etc. No charge.'

I got one reply. I called on the (very old) lady. She had a Victorian Gothic house with, at the back, the loveliest mess of a garden — not touched for years, the earth all black and yeasty with rotten leaves, etc. I was beside myself with excitement. I explained that I would get it into shape, use half for vegetables and the rest for flowers, and that I'd

supply any seeds and bulbs myself. I was dashing off to get
my spade when she caught me by the arm. 'I trust you won't
be helping yourself to the produce,' she said.

I am happy to report that within a month the lady had got
her allotment, thanks to the chair of the Middlesex
Allotments and Gardens Council, to whom I wrote on her
behalf. But should it really have been necessary for her to
be so persistent?

Few will deny that the worst allotment sites are shabby
places, especially during the winter when they are largely
deserted. The general public regards them with
disapproval, and many local authorities feel fidgety about
them. The recent Committee of Inquiry into Allotments
spent four years finding out why they were so bad, and
thinking out ways to better them. Its report gives good and
explicit advice to local authorities on how to set about the
face-lifting of existing sites and how to establish brand-
new ones for the leisure-gardening age ahead. Coventry
has made good use of that advice; Birmingham, Bristol,
Cardiff and Sheffield are following suit.

The first leisure-garden site in the country was
officially opened by Lord Sandford, of the Department of
the Environment, at Westwood Heath, Coventry. This site
has a number of attractive features. It is adorned with
flowers and clumps of shrubbery; it is served by tarmac
roads with flush kerbs; it has a number of small car parks
and rejoices in a spacious cedar-wood community building
with a meeting-room, site-secretary;s office, store for
horticultural commodities, toilets with access from inside
and out, and a children's play area. Its only material fault
is that nearly all the plots inconveniently non-rectangular.

The leisure gardens of the city of tomorrow will be
mostly peripheral, and reached by car. Plots with summer-
houses or chalets will become in effect private family
picnic sites — a substitute, perhaps, for the drive into the
country, the weekend cottage, or the rural camping site.
"The emphasis," says Professor Thorpe "should be on

good design, family, beauty, community, amenity, respectability, productivity, grow-to-show, grow-for-fun, and grow-for-leisure."

The choice of site is all-important. It is no good assuming that any piece of neglected wasteland, useless for other development, will necessarily do for allotment gardens. For example, a filled-in tip between a gasworks and a motorway, given to flooding, exposed to severe frost and a natural wind-tunnel into the bargain would not make a good site. A good one would have workable, tested soil, a gentle slope to the south, shelter from prevailing winds and an overall park-like appearance — with a pond, perhaps, or an unpolluted stream, and clumps of trees around it. Town-planners should be earmarking such sites to satisfy the predictable need of many future flat-owning and other garden-starved city-dwellers. As for the local councils, they should forthwith give the provision of leisure gardens parity with other recreational claims.

The communal areas of new leisure gardens will probably have to be the responsibility of the Parks Department; but much of the running of the site could be done by the plot-holders acting in association. And the plot-holders would obviously have to pay a fair rent. As the report says: "A substantial increase in rents will reduce the numbers who find it cheap to neglect their plots."

There are bound, of course, to be snags — lack of money, lack of drive, insecurity of tenure, and stubborn old so-and-sos (like myself) who suspect change and resist it. Like the robins we befriend on our plots, we are clamant in defence of our territorial rights, resisting anything that looks like regimentation or gimmickry, taking badly to being told to keep our heaps of muck out of sight. But we all have to accept change, because it will be for the good of ourselves and others; and we can help perhaps more than else.

The Price of a Plot Thickens

After the drought came the deluge, so that grass, ground-cover weeds, and winter greens became suddenly and wonderfully verdant. All told, we have little to complain about on our plots though we go on a bit about our neighbours, the Old Grammarians Football Club, who have put up a goal-post too near our eastern boundary. The well-booted football, they claim, rarely invades our plots more than once in a weekend match. To a gardener, however, once is too often.

But at least we have our plots, which puts us back into the "I'm all right, Jack," class. The national waiting list, I believe has now reached and passed 100,000; and 6,093 more plots were lost last year to "development."

To set against this loss there are plans for new allotment sites in some parts, including ours, under the Government's job creation schemes. Unfortunately too many of these will be temporary sites, and temporary sites are anathema to the allotment movement. How can a plot-holder be expected to put heart, back, or even ultimately feet into a plot which he or she knows will soon be lost?

The long queue of "middle class types" waiting for plots has now put the demand for them far above supply, out-pricing the pensioners. One London borough is reported to be proposing rents of £15 and £37.50 per annum, for 10 and 20 rods respectively, regardless of amenities provided. And some councils appear to be getting restive about those long twelve months of notice need to raise the rents — one of the rights of plot-holders embodied in the 1950 Allotments Act, which allows tenants to reap their full year's harvest and then withdraw gracefully and without grievance, should they be unable to unwilling to pay the increased charge.

Plot holders are not necessarily being churlish when they resist steep rent increases. They claim, and with some justification, that they are contributing to the country's economy as well as to their own, and helping our balance of payments by a considerable sum: £30M (some put it much higher) was the figure suggested by Lord Broadbridge — himself a plot-holder — in a House of Lords debate.

Birmingham, the largest of British allotment authorities, may be regarded as a model. From the beginning of this year its basic annual rent for a standard ten-rod plot (300 square yards) is to be £3.15. To this will be added charges of 40p for piped water supply, hard surfaced roadways, and flush toilets: after which we reach the realm of the leisure garden and meet the justifiably steeper charges of £1 for a tool locker, £6.50 for a summerhouse, and £12.50 for a greenhouse.

A small reduction is to be allowed for paying up within three months, and a 50 per cent reduction to all persons over the age of 65, which sounds encouragingly like fair dealing — in fact a model, as well as a warning, to those councils who might be tempted to charge excessive rents for patches of land conspicuous only by an absence of amenities and a general disarray.

The London borough of Brent also has an amenity-related rent structure. So has the city of Sheffield, which grades it allotment sites on a points system, awarding a maximum of five points for each of the following advantages: access to site, condition of avenues, soil, aspect, water supply, security against vandalism and theft, boundary fencing, car parks, toilets, community and storage huts. A score of 30–50 points rates a site grade one, and qualifies it for a higher rent.

All this information, and more, is available in periodical bulletins of the London Association of Recreational Gardeners, while the National Allotments Society (now the Society of Leisure Gardeners) issues free leaflets on such things as running gardening associations, insurance and seed-schemes.

The Department of the Environment also offers guidance in the shape of a document entitled *Model Rules As To Allotment Gardens,* which includes a model agreement form, to be signed by both the clerk of the council and the applicant. Important conditions of this agreement are that the tenant shall keep his plot in a good state of cultivation, shall not cause any nuisance and shall not underlet nor erect any building without the written consent of the council; the tenancy to be terminated by 12 months' notice by either party. For breaking rules, however, the tenant is liable to eviction after one month's notice; and any notice may be served on a tenant either personally, or by leaving it at his last known abode, or by registered letter addressed to him there, or by "fixing the same in some conspicuous manner on the allotment garden." This last must surely be the ultimate degradation for a plot holder.

Lords and Others

Allotments, to quote *Chambers Encyclopaedia,* are small plots of land let for cultivation, sometimes by private landlords but usually by local authorities, to individuals and allotment associations. They were originally provided for country labourers by their overlords, but now are found in or near towns. Many of today's dwellers are, of course, descendants of those rural labourers — those allottees to whom allotments were originally allotted.

With waiting lists of applicants running into the hundreds of thousands, it is becoming increasingly difficult, if not impossible, for aspirants to join the ranks of happy diggers. Some of the more progressive councils are making new sites, well designed and with desirable amenities; but for the rest, councils appear to be either blatantly anti-allotment from the start, or cautious about what they imagine to be merely a temporary — and perhaps fickle — demand. They are suspicious of this growing back-to-the-land search for plot and patches on which people can commune with Mother Nature as their ancestors did.

However, in looking for a plot, it is wise first to try the local council's allotment department over the telephone. The best you can hope for, alas, is to have your name added to the waiting list. But you can, in the meantime, look elsewhere, because there are such things as private - as opposed to council — allotments if you can manage to track them down.

Recently, for instance, I discovered some well administered and desirable church allotments in a nearby village. The land was — very commendably — left and endowed by a local lady who died early this century.

Official statistics in the *Thorpe Allotment Report* show that more than 3,000 country parishes have allotments, and that a quarter of them are private. They came into

48

existence in the early nineteenth century (day of dire want) when an Act of Parliament gave parish gardens the power to let up to 50 acres of land to individuals at a reasonable rent. In our village, some of the cottages built by those original allottees of a century and a half ago still stand, quaint and attractive memorials to humble enterprise, with large magnolias now growing in one or two of the front gardens.

If you happen to live near a stately home, it is possible that allotments already exist, or could be revived. Some members of the present House of Lords are acknowledged allotmenteers. So, in effect, was the Duke of Marlborough of a century ago, with something like a thousand allotments on his Oxfordshire estates.

Then there are the allotments provided (though not necessarily all tenanted) by the nationalised industries. British Rail had 75,000 individual plots in 1950, but has far fewer now.

In the good old days, porters used to be allowed to put in a bit of vegetable gardening between train arrivals, besides planting out flower beds, to compete for Smartest Station award. Only in these less gracious times — as reported recently in the *Guardian* — can a railway plot holder, an OAP, become faced with a rent rise of 3,000 per cent. In our parts, some people whose back gardens abut on the railway are able, at a price, to turn over the intervening grass for food production.

The National Coal Board also has allotments; and since miners are said these days to prefer golf to gardening (and why shouldn't they?) there may be a few vacant plots in attractive and agriculturally productive parts of the country — Nottinghamshire, for instance, in the neighbourhood of Sherwood Forest and Byron's fabulous Newstead Abbey. British Waterways have some alongside canals, which seems a good place for gardening in dry spells, with possibilities of growing water cress and water lilies, and have the occasional swim. Private industries, factories and garden villages sometimes make plots available to their workers and to people living nearby.

To the truly determined, in fact, a potential plot might not be far to seek. To those living within sight of fields, a farmer might, under a gentleman's agreement, allow the use of a corner patch. (There are examples — going back through the centuries — of enterprising individuals renting a field from a farmer, dividing it into plots, and sub-letting them at a profit.) Within towns, on a crop and share basis, some old person's neglected garden might profitably be brought back into cultivation.

But with more clear cut aims and less empirical methods, gardeners' associations with a feasible site in mind can be formed by calling an open meeting, choosing a worthy chair, and electing secretary, treasurer, and a committee. For this, the National Society of Leisure Gardeners (the old National Allotments and Gardens Society) can help with advice and a leaflet entitled Allotment Associations — how to form and run them.

They also publish a little marvel in the shape of a pocket *Gardeners' Companion and Diary*, clearly produced, modestly priced, of excellent practical value, and including all essential information about forming and running an association, duties of officers, conduct of meetings, digest of allotment law and much else.

Rabbits

During the wet winter weeks there was little incentive to go to our allotments, with the result that freely ranging wild rabbits took up residence under our sheds. They ate off the leek tops for starters. Our longest serving plot-holder says he has never known this to happen before — always sprouts and cabbages, he says, with the leeks left untouched. Until recently Paddy, our veteran plot holder, was given the shooting rights by the Council. Regularly at dawn he confronted the rabbits at early breakfast. His trusty dog had only three legs but was the equal, Paddy affirmed, of any rival with four. But alas, Paddy has now gone from us, suddenly, in his sleep; and his grieving widow — an animal lover — has impounded the gun, they say.

The only non-violent defence against rabbits, it seems, is a wire or nylon net cage or cover. One of our old timers claims partial success with string (we call it band in these parts) soaked in creosote and tied to stakes around the vulnerable vegetables.

My plot neighbour, Nelson, however, has produced a can of Renardine. Instructions are to place strings dressed with it on sticks alongside the garden, nine inches from the ground. To protect young peas and beans, you arrange these strings beside the rows, three inches from the ground. Or you can pour the objectionable stuff on fine sawdust and sprinkle this around plants. But it is not pleasant to handle, and should be used, if at all, with care. And if it rains hard, you might have been wasting your time.

Nelson declares that we shall never get rid of our rabbits until we all raise our garden huts a foot off the ground and so prevent the invaders from breeding underneath in undisturbed comfort. They make their burrows, he tells me, about an arm's length into the ground under the sheds or into any available heap or mound. There they make a cosy nest, lined with fur and grass, ready to receive the naked young.

I'm told that a lad who owns a ferret has offered to solve our rabbit problem for us. Meanwhile, however, a more serious threat hangs over the less prosperous members of our fraternity.

During those dreadful depression years of half a century ago, the Society of Friends took the initiative in raising funds to assist unemployed victims of the depression to take on allotments and receive gifts of seeds and fertilisers. Tens of thousands of families were helped in this way. The Quakers helped to found and organise the National Allotments Society, which is celebrating its fiftieth birthday this year in an apprehensive frame of mind.

Allotments, outside wartime, have always been vulnerable. Now rents are going up again. On our enclave the increase amounts to 25 per cent by my calculation, but 33.3 according to Taffy, our longest serving plot holder, who is a retired maths teacher and ought to know. This recurrent raising of rents has become a habit and, like the man in Chekhov reflecting on his marriage, we are getting used to it. But Nelson, who is on the site almost daily to take the allotmenteering pulse, says that many speak of giving up their plots, and this is what some "anti allotment councils" are accused of wanting to happen.

The spring bulletin of the National Society forecasts the doubling, and more than doubling, of rents in some places. And worse — one council (Cheltenham) is reported to have decided to sell off some of its allotment land; if so, that authority seems to have jumped the gun. Because a glimmer of light has appeared on the horizon which might herald a brighter day for allotmenteers. The Government is withdrawing the provision in the Local Government Planning and Land Bill to allow councils to dispose of statutory allotment land without reference to the Secretary of State for the Environment.

Under the existing Allotment Acts we have certain protective rights given by a succession of grateful and understanding Governments back in the days of the two World Wars, in the fever of digging of victory, and since. These rights need to be retained, especially now that we appear to be on the brink of digging for survival. Currently, however, we see them being whittled away. When local authorities charge rents which may not be "reasonable" and shorten considerably the legal twelve months' notice to quite or to raise rents, the law is so vague that High Court rulings have to be sought by the victims.

Unlike many European countries, we lack an overall guiding plan, or policy, or money to make allotments places of recreational and economic value, though Professor Thorpe and his committee of Inquiry into Allotments set up in 1965, did in fact point the way. The *Thorpe Report* did not always please the conservative and fundamentally practical man on the plot who saw in it some cloud-cuckoo land ideas and some unacceptable window dressing. He was suspicious of its suggestion that all the hoary old Allotment Acts should be scrapped in favour of one brand new one. Nor could be stomach the recommendation that leisure garden should replaced the beloved and time-endeared name of allotment. He could tell Professor Thorpe (and did) that leisure gardens and allotments are two different animals, as different as French Poodles and Old English Sheepdogs.

Nevertheless, the *Thorpe Report* has much that is good in it, and if updated it could serve us well, particularly if we uphold the contention that allotment gardening should be regarded as a recreation and treated as such. There is a glimmer of hope in the words uttered by the Minister for Local Government and Environmental Services. "At present," he said, "we are considering comprehensive legislation to take in the *Thorpe Report*. There has been in the background of the Government's thinking for some time what is called a Recreational Gardening Bill..."

The Plot, the Law, and the Class Factor

Most of our forebears lived by and from the land. They lived a rural life and had daily contact with the soil. Then — a couple of centuries or so ago — land enclosures sent them into the industrial towns for work; but even then they sought a bit of land to cultivate on the edges of those new towns. The reason, I would guess, was quite as much the need to get out of the factories and foundries for fresh air and relaxation as the need to supplement poor wages for large families. Nevertheless, allotment gardening at low rents came to be considered as a dole for the labouring poor, helping them, by their own honest sweat, to eke out an often miserable existence.

From then on, allotments were never quite respectable among the better-off, and this attitude still lingers, even though plotholders today include a large number of academics, professional and sedentary workers seeking recreation by gentle cultivation of, and communion with, the land. Eventually, therefore, it is to be hoped that to have an allotment will cease to be *declassé*. The process would certainly be accelerated if some face-lifting could be put promptly into action on those sites which have become eyesores both to the plotholders themselves and to the neighbouring public.

The allotment fraternity believes that much of the blame lies with local authorities. Far from initiating renovatory activities, some of them are suspected of deliberately neglecting allotment sites — making them less attractive to would-be tenants, and, by an unreasonable raising of rents, pricing them out of popularity in order to sell the land to developers. Incidentally, the Central Council of Physical Recreation has similar fears about sports fields being sold for commercial purposes — hence Mr John Carlisle's private members' Sports Field and Recreational Facilities Bill.

It was the Thorpe *Allotments Report* of 1969 that made recommendations for an improved status of allotment gardening so as to stop the rot and point the way forward. It suggested, in the first place, that all existing allotment Acts (there were quite a few) should be rejected and replaced by a brand new Act which would retain the good and reject the bad.

But so far as the plotholder was concerned, the old Acts had given protective rights — a reward for Dig-for-Victory loyalty in two world wars; he or she was inclined to smell a rat at any suggestion of abolishing them. Nor did the old timer, nurtured perhaps on a Protestant work ethic, take kindly to the report's recommendation that, in future, allotments should be styled a "leisure garden." Leisure rhymed with pleasure and had connotations of indolence and hedonism.

So the plotholder — or the allotment society — must shoulder some of the blame for the statement that followed the 1969 *Thorpe Report*. Tom Hume, however, a founder member, secretary and allotment consultant of the London Association of Recreational Gardeners formed in 1974, saw the value of the report from the outset. So, now, do hundreds of thousands of allotment holders throughout England and Wales. Glyn Jones, secretary of the National Society of Allotment and Leisure Gardeners tells me he is trying to get his many members put in the picture.

Tom Hume played a substantial part in drafting the new Recreational Gardening Bill, introduced in the House of Lords by Lord Wallace of Coslany, president of the London Association of Recreational Gardeners and a one time allotmenteer.

That was in January 1984. It reached the Commons in July, but its sponsor, Nigel Spearing, realising the government intended to oppose it in its present form, withdrew it. An amended Bill was re-introduced by Lord Wallace on December 3. It reached and passed the Committee stage this January and, following a third reading on February 18, was passed and sent to the Commons — "to the dangerous waters of another place," as Lord Wallace put it. Lord Graham, in congratulating him, spoke of "the valuable contribution that he has made for millions of people who rely upon some improved framework for their allotment work in the future."

The Bill's main aim is to raise the status of allotment gardening and establish it, in law, as a recreation on a par with other recreations that local authorities fund and foster. Section 19(1)(b) of the Local Government (Miscellaneous Provisions) Act of 1976 empowers local authorities to provide outdoor recreational facilities "consisting of pitches for team games, athletic grounds, swimming pools, tennis courts, cycle tracks, golf courses, bowling greens, riding schools, camp sites, and facilities for gliding." The intention is to have the words "allotment gardens" inserted after "camp sites." Beyond that, the intent is to put allotment gardening on a sound and secure basis from which it can develop and help to meet some of today's urgent social needs.

Tom Hume, who has always been reluctant to let the good points of the *Thorpe Report* sink into oblivion, now urges us to write to our MPs to support the Bill, if and when it is debated in the House of Commons later this year.*

Whilst this particular Bill is long-gone, why not write to your MP now in support of allotments?

Plotting for the Good Life

In the 1960s there were many vacant garden allotment; in the 1970s, long waiting lists for them. Today, judging by reports, we have see-sawed back on the side of untenanted plots, particularly in the South-East. Suggested reasons are many and varied: we are less muscular than our forebears; we are losing our traditional attachment to the soil; we have become sports-crazed and passive telly-addicts; as car owners we are more mobile; we are put off by high rents and poor facilities. And so on. Nelson, my octogenarian plot associate, a countryman who believes hard work is good for you, has always maintained that people today are shy of even a little manual labour.

In February Lord Wallace of Coslany, president of the London Association of Recreational Gardeners, broached the matter of vacant plots in the House of Lords. He asked Lord Young to what extent Manpower Services schemes include horticultural training and cultivation of produce on vacant local authority allotment plots.

The minister pointed out that those vacant plots were the responsibility of the local authorities, but that 11,000 YTS training places were available in 1985-6 covering horticulture and agriculture, and that with the Job Training Scheme he hoped there would be many more. "I am quite sure that in themselves allotments are a very good thing," he added somewhat enigmatically, though one noble lord volunteered that the capacity to dig an allotment is limited to heroes, and not a fair test for a YTS youngster — which perhaps proves Nelson's point.

Mr Lawrence Hills of the Henry Doubleday Research Association, now located at the National Centre for Organic Gardening near Coventry, is concerned about the over-50s who have become redundant and for whom co-operative organic ventures might be a good thing on some of those vacant plots. Mr Hills started a directory of vacant plots in the 1985, and early 1986, HDRA newsletters. He can see the good sense in setting up organic projects and co-operatives on unused allotments, thus saving the sites from those rapacious property developers.

It was Mr Jack Moon, a Kent old age pensioner, however, who has actually devised and outlined a detailed gardening project for the unemployed. With the encouragement of Mr Hills and help from other quarters, he managed last October, to get his project going at Sidcup in the borough of Bexley. It is being funded by the Manpower Services Commission and administered by the community programme managers of Parkhill Community Projects. The participants in this project, male and female, are enthusiastic, he tells me. The site impressed the Mayor of Bexley when he visited it. Approval and support also appeared in local papers.

When the one year scheme is completed, it is hoped that the participants will form the nucleus of a workers' co-operative to supply the growing market in organic produce. The Manpower Services Commission is monitoring this project and, if successful, will consider extending it to the Bromley area where Mr Moon lives. He is secretary of the Elmstead Lane Allotment Association at Chislehurst. He rather hopes the idea might spread nationwide.

Bromley borough council has shown some enterprise by issuing 10,000 copies of a leaflet devised by local allotmenteers, advertising their allotment vacancies and putting forward the undeniable advantages of "Taking a share in the Good Life with an allotment in Bromley" as they put it. The leaflet has a map of the borough showing the 52 allotment sites from Penge to Orpington and Chislehurst to Biggin Hill. Most of the sites are now run by associations which either have taken leases of the land or which administer the sites on behalf of the council. These are uniting in the Amalgamated Allotments Associations (AAA).

The Chislehurst site to which Mr Moon is attached took over management on January 1, joined the AAA, and had 11 vacant plots taken up in a few weeks. There remain a few sites where plots can be rented direct from the council. Bee keeping and vine growing can be found on some plots in this garden corner of England.

In response to a recent question about vacant plots, a member of the BBC *Gardeners' Question Time* team suggested that gardening should figure more prominently in school life. I agree. I can recall may own primary school in Oxfordshire during the First World War where the school garden on the sunlit valley side brought fresh air and freedom on one afternoon a week. The school's stock punishment, I remember, was to deprive us of our gardening afternoon, which was sufficient to concentrate our minds and improve our behaviour.

Mr Denis Midgely has a caravan at Hornsea, East Yorkshire, and an allotment with vacant plots around him He sent me a plan of his rose and raised vegetable beds, similar to those of Bill Masser, the Eton maths master whose gardening activities I referred to recently. Mr Midgely wonders if summer caravanners could be persuaded to take on these vacant plots as "leisure" gardens, or looked-after "wild" gardens, or even "forest" gardens like the model forest garden on Mr Robert Hart's farm at Wenlock Edge, described as a miniature reproduction of the self-maintaining ecosystem of the natural forest, consisting entirely of fruit and nut trees and bushes, perennial and self-seeding vegetables, and culinary and medicinal herbs.*

See Robert Hart: Forest Gardens. Resurgence Books 1991.

The Shape of Things to Come

During the quiet anticyclonic days of November, those of us who escaped the storm havoc, and who had freedom of choice, spent the tranquil hours of dwindling daylight on our plots and found plenty to do. The needful jobs on an allotment stare balefully back at you. There is no escaping them. To try to elude them is to carry a heavy conscience and worry about unfairness to well kept plots around you. How I miss Nelson.

First, with firm resolve, sword-sharp spade, and garden line, I trimmed and straightened all path and boundary edges, leaving gutters or runnels to help with drainage, and giving the plot a renewed recognisable shape and entity.

Next, having already decided in Nelson's absence to abolish general all-over digging for an experimental year, I have proceeded — by way of minimum concession to orthodoxy — to dig four deepish trenches, and plan to dig a fifth. (We have a good depth of topsoil.) Taken at easy stages this trenching was no great task, given the mild and pleasant weather in which it was done: though my excavatory endeavours did lead one passing plot holder to inquire whether I was burying someone.

The job done, I paused to ask myself why I had done it, and what advantages would accrue, demanding convincing answers. To begin with, I argued that I had exposed slugs, bugs, grubs, wireworms, and other soil pests for my robin and other co-operative wildlife to forage for, breakfast beakily on, attack by tooth, catch by claw, or otherwise inelegantly annihilate. Following this gift to some of my creatures great and small, I made sprinklings of potash and superphosphate in and around the bared soil of the trenches for their better health and fitness; and since the trenches were dug near rows of winter cabbage, kale and sprouts, some of the upturned soil served to buttress and protect the sometimes leaning and listing brassicas.

I also reminded myself of the benefits that frosts can bring to upturned clods of earth, crumbling them and at the same time making living conditions difficult for any remaining soil pests. The trenches themselves will receive acceptable rotting vegetation and compost through the winter, to be filled over with earth in early spring, and made ready for leguminous plants in April and May — runner beans, mangetout peas, and an indispensable row of sweet peas.

A few of our plots have become vacant, perhaps of recent vandalism which shocked some of us who thought we were immune. Vacant allotments seem to be widespread these days, which is a great pity because getting away from concrete and clutter to work close to the soil fulfils some natural need in us and would bring satisfaction to many of those who would give it a trial.

So why are plots vacant, we may ask. Professor Harry Thorpe and his Committee of Inquiry into Allotments were asking themselves the same question back in 1965 (when vandalism had scarcely been invented) and continued trying to find an answer up to 1969 when the *Allotments Report* of 460 pages was published.

The Inquiry was appointed "To review general policy on allotments in the light of present day conditions in England and Wales and to recommend what legislative and other changes, if any, are needed." They went to extraordinary lengths to acquaint themselves with basic information; visited allotment sites; read up allotment history to find that it originated in pauperism and continued as provision for the poor; distributed long and complicated questionnaires; mugged up the diversity of Allotment Acts of Parliament; and invited studies to investigate allotments in 49 different areas and wrote final theses with attached distribution maps, graphs and other tabulated data.

It is not difficult to imagine bright-faced young students, finding the open air a pleasant change from the classroom, striding on to a plot and demanding of an old codger like... "Hello, Dad, tell us how old are you? How long you've had this path of dirt? And what do they make you pay for it?" To quote from the report itself, "Some of the questions might with advantage have been asked in a different way."

To be fair, however, the students must have done a useful, if a little too entangled, a job. They found "anti-allotment atmosphere" and "haphazard administration" in some local authority offices whilst the "them and us" old guard on the plots reacted unfavourably — they had grown to regard allotments as the rightful preserve of the "labouring classes" free from interlopers calling allotments leisure gardens.

Reasons for vacant plots then — in descending order of frequency — were given as death, illness, old age, lost interest, moving from district, weed invasion, insecurity of tenure, vandalism with theft.

The *Thorpe Report* was so comprehensive and penetrating, and reached such strong recommendations for improvement, that governments possibly find it forbidding. Perhaps there should have been an honest-to-goodness plotholder on that committee to keep things simple. It would be interesting to hear reflective comments from those who were actually on it — say Frances Perry or jolly Bill Snelson (Major H.S.E. Snelson OBE).

To try to put it in a nutshell, the allotment tangle probably derives from the fact that gardeners are for the most part individualists, sometimes indeed loners, self-contained, following their own bent, interfering with no one; whereas ideally, allotment holders need to be communally minded, friendly, and outgoing, sharing, conforming, co-operative people, living in a classless allotment world.

A Good Plot Wears Thin

Being, as you might say, something of an old buffer, I can remember quite vividly the outbreak of the First World War. I was swinging on the garden gate when a man came across the road to break the news to my father.

Tomatoes were ripening, I remember, against the warm stone wall of the house. We called them love apples. Wartime shortages were soon upon us and we relied quite heavily on our allotment.

After the 1908 Allotment Act, plots became available to all. Previously they had been reserved for deserving members of the "labouring poor." There were about half a million allotments in England and Wales when war broke out, many of them in Oxfordshire. My father had one of them. I used to help — or hinder — him, watering the rhubarb and treading on seedlings. Also, as the war and my age advanced, by way of doing my bit to vary our diet I used to go crayfishing with friends in the stream that feeds the Blenheim Park Lake.

In memory, at least, my childhood was idyllic — the sun always shone, the meadows were rich with wild flowers, robins built their nests in discarded kettles and glow-worms, buried in grassy banks, shone at night.

The recent weeks of blue skies and brilliant sunshine brought these memories flooding back as I toiled to keep the crops happy and weeds down on my plot.

I battle daily with the bindweed, hoping in vain to thwart it. New shoots ceaselessly pop up. Only after reading John Clare – that peasant poet of the countryside, belatedly commemorated in Poet's Corner the other day – did I relent somewhat. In a strictly limited area I am allowing it to climb tall canes, giving it equal opportunity with the beans and sweet peas. It races up with buds at every leaf joint, soon to "lift athirst their tender throated flowers/Agape for dew falls and for honey showers"... as Clare has it.

63

Poor John Clare. He was set to work at seven, labouring beside his ballad-singing father, grew up to write poetry, fell in love with daughters of disapproving parents, was lionised, befriended by men of letters, and entertained by the nobility, but preferred to dine in the servants' hall.

According to the *Dictionary of National Biography,* it was when the wife of the Bishop of Peterborough took him to see the Merchant of Venice at the theatre that he was "struck by a fit of insanity" which signalled his eventual impoverished end.

John Clare witnessed the field enclosures that robbed the peasants of their independence, land and rights, and him of nature rambles.

On sunny summer weekends, when activity, friendliness and jocularity abound on our plots, I sometimes go romantic and wonder if those old-time open fields presented a similar picture to ours. Clad in russet brown, wielding clumsy and sometimes murderous-looking implements so unlike the refined tools of today, they must have felt the benefits of open air and homegrown food, felt similar joys and sorrows, and made the most of what they'd got, as we do.

The security of allotments today is as tenuous as that of field strips at the time of the enclosures. The million and a half allotments at the end of the First World War dwindled again to half a million. A similar pattern followed the Second World War.

Today there are reported to be so many vacant plots in some areas that holders fear takeover by ever-eager property developers offering enticing inducements.

Readers with such fears write asking for advice which I feel helpless to give, apart from suggesting they talk to sympathetic councillors, write protesting letters to newspapers or to a worthy and greenish MP, approach Friends of the Earth, or seek advice from the secretary of the National Society of Allotment and Leisure Gardeners.

Sod's Law

At this time of year when allotments are sodden and unkind, it is wise to keep off them, to let the wildlife and chickweed take over, to sit back in warm comfort and ruminate — worry, even — about the sorrowful history of allotments and about their uncertain future.

A rumour is rife that our own allotment site will soon be used by property developers to enlarge our village which already claims to be the largest in the country. It has a strong sense of community and a magnificent medieval church in Tadcaster stone, tastefully floodlit at Christmas time.

Since most of our forebears lived off the land, it is not surprising that some of us feel an innate right to dig and delve on small patches of this common earth that are loaned to us. Twenty years ago, following years of neglect and lack of enthusiasm, our plots were suddenly all under spade, with a long waiting list at the council offices. On that occasion, a rumour that we were to be dispossessed and the land returned to market gardening brought us smartly up to attention.

But there was an additional reason. Allotments were in the news in 1970. Professor Harry Thorpe of Birmingham University had just published his bulky allotments report, showing us how to drag our old style allotments into the modern world, give them a face lift, remove the old bedsteads, tin baths, and rickety sheds; how to make them look wanted rather than looked at askance by the public at large.

Our allotments certainly began as a dole for the deserving poor — for the erstwhile peasant farmers who had been dispossessed by those deplorable enclosure acts that drove people off the land into the new factory towns or on to the parish poor relief. Our village, now prosperous, had its Pauper Gardens almost two centuries ago; a 12-acre field was divided into 20 equal parts and allotted to the most deserving poor with the largest families — but on threat of eviction for misbehaviour. Some of the tiny one-storey cottages (mercifully renamed New Village) survived with a kind of charm until a year or so ago — one of them with a splendid magnolia blooming at the door.

Not all was servile acquiescence however. There were those who showed their mettle. Gerrard Winstanley in Commonwealth times, for example. Born in Wigan in 1609 but moving to London, he was able to educate himself, to write tracts in the style of Milton and dedicate them to his "beloved countrymen of the Countie of Lancaster."

Was the Earth, he asked, "made to preserve a few covetous men for them to live at ease and for them to bag and barn up the treasures of the Earth from others, that these may beg and starve in a fruitful land; or was it made to preserve all her children?"

In the spring of 1649 — a year of depression in England, and also the year King Charles I lost his head — the Diggers under Winstanley had their brief glory. In several parts of the country they dug up common land, planted vegetables for all, and invited the locals to join them.

At St George's Hill, 40 diggers were at work, declaring that 5,000 would soon join them. This was too much for the local property owners who became aggressive, beat up the innocent Diggers, burned their sheds, destroyed their tools, and sent for the troops to evict them. It was not until 1919 that allotments became available to all, and not until 1970 did the middle classes discover allotments.

Thus in 1970 on our own site as elsewhere, we watched the influx of new tenants — a cross-section of the community from amateur gardeners and vegetarians among the professional classes to the stolid villagers whose forbears had always been close to the land. To begin with, it was an uneasy mix, but things soon settled into camaraderie.

Culture

Ground Rules

My allotment, acquired almost a quarter of a century ago
in pleasant surroundings, is a reasonably level, gently
south-facing strip, 30 yards by 10, with a hawthorn hedge
at its west end as protection against strong westerlies that
cross the country from the Atlantic. At the eastern end is
a thick, summer-emblazoned potentilla hedge, which gives
a little shelter from cold winter easterlies that probably
originate in Siberia.

The crop rows run mostly north and south across the
plot to get the benefit of sunlight on both sides through
the day. This enables them to avoid lop-sidedness or a
misshapen stance.

There were plenty of plots to choose from in the late
Sixties — a time of allotment depression because cars and
TV sets had become popular for weekend jaunts and
sedentary sport watching. And thus I, an allotment novice,
proved lucky in my choice, once my wife and I had cleared
the wilderness and installed civilisation.

Today, given a choice, I should know exactly what to
ask myself in looking for a plot, given that I was
conversant with the climate and weather of the district. Is
the plot fairly level with deep workable soil? Good. Has it
an open aspect and satisfactory drainage? Even better.
Has it some fence or hedge shelter from prevailing winds?
Good again. Do the crops look healthy or, if the plot is
untenanted, do the weeds look happy? Very happy.

And what of the plotholders themselves? Are they
friendly? Cooperative? Communicative? Encouraging?
Helpful? Almost certainly they are, so long as you are
adequately self-effacing at first, willing to listen and learn,
and law-abiding.

So you sign your contract, pay your rent and, in effect,
become lord or lady of your domain. In signing, you have
probably agreed not to put barbed wire round your plot,

not to mine it for minerals, nor to build a permanent structure thereon. Since you had no intention of doing anything of the kind, but rather intend to enjoy the fresh air, healthy exercise, chummy companionship, and to cultivate the soil with diligence and delight, you are off to a good start.

Back in more feudal times, it was sometimes forbidden to be at your allotment on Sundays, or after 6am on workdays, or to till your plot with anything but a spade, or to grow flowers. Things have improved somewhat, though the allotment societies have never in their history, I think, demonstrated with placards to get better treatment.

With the contract signed, the rent paid and informal introductions made, you think of the needful garden tools — spade and fork mostly, with a hoe and a rake, a trowel and dibber for good measure.

Primitive people no doubt managed with flat stones, animal shoulder blades, deer antlers, and digging sticks. As a last resort they probably went to ground with their own hands and heels for tools, as can sometimes be seen even today. During World War II in southern Italy, I remember seeing peasants breaking clods with the heavy two-pronged bidente while on the next hillside beasts of burden were urged on.

The spade has been in use over many centuries, first perhaps in ancient China. Its shape and design have changed little, whether made in bronze, iron, or the splendid stainless steel of today. In some countries a long-handled straight spade is preferred for its greater leverage in heavier land; on others a short-handled implement with a tapered, curved, or square blade, perhaps at a slight angle to the shaft.

The dutch thrust, or shimmy hoe (as opposed to the pull hoe), which I find so useful for infant weed assassination in spring, appears to be unknown in some countries.

A rotovator is not to be recommended on an allotment. It tears up the underground bindweed and couch grass

70

into thousands of root cuttings which quickly spring to life with great vigour.

My allotment shed contains some 19th-century tools left behind by Nelson, my one-time octogenarian plot associate. They were probably inherited from his grandfather. These are hoe-like tools of varying shape, of ponderous weight, and long shafted. Today we are fortunate to have a wide range of stainless steel garden tools available.

There are other matters to be aware of in selecting an allotment. Is there a water tap nearby? Can hosepipes be used? Is there a rain tub, and are there gutters on the shed roof? Are any pests or diseases prevalent? Is the soil acid, alkaline, or neutral? This will decide what you can successfully grow. Is there wild life, apart from the robin which will be there to greet you when you arrive?

You will quickly become aware of the reasonable priced fertiliser Growmore at the allotment store. It has equal proportions of N, P and K nutrients (nitrogen, phosphate and potash). If you intend to be organic, you will save all your kitchen waste for the compost heap, explore other organic fertilisers, and hope for a farmer who will deliver you a load of vintage farmyard manure.

Breath of Fresh Air

One of my ever-fresh childhood memories is of newly-hatched chicks, early in the year, drying out in the fireglow, welcoming the warmth, and chirping in chorus as my mother saw to their comfort. Every year this image recurs as I sow my half-hardy annuals in the airing cupboard to germinate, which they quickly do — chirping for all I know — to undetected decibels.

And now spring has arrived with a hiccup or two and a wealth of early blossom. It is good to be out in the open air. All our allotments appear to be taken, with some new and younger faces. We welcome them all.

No longer are allotments the preserve of us old timers, nor are they for men only. More women are now on the plots, often married couples, making the scene more cheerful and friendly.

Some of the younger newcomers might welcome bits of advice, if given with discretion, to break and rake the soil to a fine tilth, for instance, before sowing the unimpeded seed to hasten slowly. Not to sow till the soil is warm enough and moist. To sow thinly, with care, and later to thin out — the smaller the seed, the shallower the drill — carrots, beetroot, and leeks about three-quarter inch deep, beans twice as deep, and peas rather less. And don't forget the label and any details. In fact put the marker in first to get it right.

If dry, water. If wet, keep off the soil. If the wildlife is active, take protective measures with wire guards, netting, cloches, sticks, and cotton. (The rabbits are varying their diet by eating the Japanese onion tops on my plot this year.) Don't sow more than you need. A little and often is a good tip with quickly maturing crops like lettuce, radishes, spring onions and Swiss chard.

My potatoes — a small quantity of Concorde, Kondor, Romano, and Charlotte — are trenched with compost about five-inches deep. My Fen Globe onions are at the ready.

Rhubarb is a good crop, liking the openness of allotments, and most appreciated just now. To pull it, you slide your thumb down the inside of the stem to the base, then press and pull it away from the crown. Gathering should cease in July because of the accumulation of oxalic salts in the stems, but you should leave your untidy rhubarb to die down naturally and be thankful for your fruity stop gap just now.

Your rasps should have been topped, and big bud removed from blackcurrants and burnt. Gooseberries need potash, pruning, and opening out.

Mulching is the buzz word today because of possible water shortage — but only after rain. It controls weeds and retains the moisture. But it has to be thick to be effective. Straw and leaf mould are acceptable. Carpet and black plastic are not, on aesthetic grounds. Newspaper and cardboard, only when covered by leaves and leaf mould. It is wise to eat green vegetables young and fresh, a good reason for growing your own. Sow parsnips and radishes together — the one slow growing, the other rapid, and mark the row.

Cauliflowers are greedy feeders. Benlate checks mildew. Tomatoes will ripen towards Christmas if kept watchfully in a drawer. Carrots and parsnips won't transplant.

Finally, have a care for your own safety. There is so much work to be done just know that it is easy to be neglectful of simple precautions like treading on an upturned rake. A recent communication from the Department of Trade and Industry warned that over 300,000 people were injured last year in their gardens, needing hospital treatment. A moment's thought assures me, however, that only a small proportion of these occurred on allotments because hedge trimmers, compost shredders, motor mowered power tools do not normally disturb the noiseless tenor of our way on the plots.

Nevertheless it was by a stroke of irony that the day before this warning arrived, I clumsily fell with a thud and a purple bruise, and was unable to get up unaided. Fortunately Ron from a neighbouring plot ran to help me to my feet, and Arnold from another volunteered some expert gardening help, to ease the pressure of the season's activities and make me doubly cautious. Long live the camaraderie of the allotments!

Gardener's Weather

If you are a "small" gardener, and have known the more arid parts of Africa or sun-scorched Italy, you will be grateful — up to a point — for rain-soaked England.

Nothing reconciles one more quickly and comfortably to the English climate than to possess an allotment. Or so it seems to me. In the days when I used to think of a garden as somewhere to sit in summer — which was for all my so-called working life — I was often, like many others, disappointed in the English weather, if that is not an understatement. One could rarely bask in the shade, as in an American summer. One had either to scorch in sun, if and when it appeared, or shiver in shadow; except on rare halcyon days of high barometric pressure.

It was when I retired that I discovered an important fact. An English garden is not a place to be sitting in, but to be busy in. Especially if it is an allotment — which, of course, is more a place for leeks and rhubarb than for lawns and roses. An allotment can change your whole outlook on life, and your whole outlook on the weather; at least it has mine.

Every morning of my "working life," I had pushed back the bedroom curtains at dawn of day to look out on the weather prospects. More often than not, these were bleak. Day after day I would recoil at the sight of drizzle descending from leaden clouds, and groan in desperation at the day's dim promise. And even now, conditioned by long habit, I predispose myself to groan on seeing the first grim light of day. But benignity quickly supervenes as I think how the brassicas on the allotment will enjoy the drizzle on their leaves, and how the moisture will collect on them in tiny globules and pearls of glistening splendour.

"What is the weather like?" asks my wife sleepily.

"Good for gardening," I say, as I dress with determination and issue forth, allotment-bound, and suitably clad against the elements; happy in the thought that I, too, could have stayed in bed had I wished.

On the way to the allotment one passes the time of day to other early risers. "Dreadful weather," they say. "But good for gardens," I reply. "And more rain to come," they add. "Hope so," I say, hurrying on.

But an allotment holder sometimes eats words as well as produce. At least, I do. That deluge, for instance. For two whole days I couldn't get near my plot; and when I did, it was to see just how wanton the capricious elements had been. My grand gateway of Indian corn at the entrance to the plot was knocked askew; some of the runner bean clumps down the sides of the central path were flattened to the ground with their eight-foot canes beside them; the sweet peas in the flower patch were decimated, the ridge cucumber dying, the young marrows rotting; and the wheel-barrow was full to the brim with an unwanted reservoir of water.

There was only one thing on the credit side — to speak euphemistically; and that concerned the parsnips. For weeks I had been trying in vain to dig up a boiling of parsnips but the roots go deep into their native earth. They were two feet long, and firmly entrenched. After the deluge, it was just possible to dig them out.

Of course, there are some allotment holders who say you should keep off your land in bad weather. I never contradict them. After all, I'm only a novice; I know my place. It's not for me to pontificate. But I will say this; if you insist on planting your vegetables in long rows, and have to trample the wet ground between the rows, then of course you will do harm. But why not plant vegetables in clumps (Capability Brown-wise) or in patches, say of a square yard, surrounded by little paths to be heavy-footed on.

Take, for instance, a square yard of carrots, equivalent perhaps to one row. You would sow it broadcast, as in the good old days, and watch it growing from infancy, smothering the weeds that tried to share the patch. A few aggressive carrots, you would notice, would grow at the expense of their neighbours, stealing more of their share of sustenance from the good earth, and waxing stout and strong. These you would pull and eat first (and serve them right, too) leaving room for the others to develop until, at last, the most overcrowded weaklings would have room to become spoiled and overfed darlings. Thus a steady progression of carrots would be maintained throughout the year.

It is perhaps a pity that Capability Brown gave his entire life to beautifying the vast acres (whole wapentakes almost) surrounding those eighteenth-century stately homes. Our debt to him might have been even greater if he had devoted a little of his undoubted genius to the designing of his own back garden. He would, I feel sure, have ousted the fashion of planting vegetables in long rows, as being too formal and Italianate. He would have planted them in clumps, reached by labyrinthine paths.

And he would never have minded the rain.

A Place for Children

One day, when I was working on my allotment, the peace was suddenly shattered by a sharp parental cry: "Get off and keep off!" A few moments later a small boy, head lowered, arms hanging rigid, hurried for the exit gate, muttering to himself, no doubt – since infants, I understand, now swear – "You can keep your bloody allotment!"

This made me wonder whether it is always original sin that makes older boys kick footballs into flowerbeds or ride bicycles over the begonias. Dad's short temper may be to blame; or his blinkered dedication.

Which is a pity; because, when you come to think of it, a garden is as good a place as any for children to be in. Setting aside boisterous play (as children sometimes do) where better to indulge their innate curiosity? They can observe the life-styles of growing plants and insects; explore the pattern and structure of seeds, stems, leaves, and flowers; and submit themselves to a garden's natural discipline. Small children, fascinated by gardens, are always keen to "help".

During the summer I had the company of two small children on my plot. It was a rejuvenating experience. I confess to some feeling of trepidation at the start, but when the holiday was over and those two bundles of energy had departed, a silent gloom pervaded my plot. It was a week or more before I had readjusted to a tortoise-slow pace and a close-like hush.

The presence of children in a garden can be both electric and charming. They talk incessantly, ask rapid-fire questions (which deserve honest, breathless answers), rush from one job to another, show a disfavour for using paths, plead to be allowed to water the rain-soaked lettuces, and insist on being shown how to use all tools and appliances — especially the garden rake, which is their favourite, and also the most difficult to use.

It was on her first visit to the plot that my five-year-old grand-daughter confronted me with two uplifted round blue eyes and, addressing me by my first name (to put us on level ground), delivered her ultimatum: "Keep me busy, Michael, or I'll smack your bottom."

I was, as they say, nonplussed. Fortunately, however, her seven-year-old brother at my side was not at all taken aback. Quick as thought, he pulled out three weeds (real ones), offered them to her, and said "Look Catherine; run down the path, right to the end, and put these weeds on the rubbish heap; and by the time you get back I'll have three more ready." With whoops of joy she was off, starting a lengthy stint which kept her busy, freed me from the threatened sanction, and relieved the plot of some weed infestation. What's more, my grandson and I were able to continue the "men's work" on which we were engaged. The moral is that children should be allowed to be busy in the garden, with a business suited to their age.

Ideally (repeat ideally) children would have their own small gardens, abutting on the main garden but partly secluded from it, with a tree to climb, shady corners in which to hide, a pool to play in, and a play-house large enough to hold a table at which to eat sandwiches prepared from their own home-grown lettuce, mustard and cress. All credit to the public parks who often make imaginative provision for children in play-areas — though a private garden, however small, could, for most children, be something rather special.

Miss Gertrude Jekyll, that great gardener at the turn of the century, understood children as well as gardens and wrote a book about both. It was her view that children should be given a garden ready made, and preferably in autumn. (There may be purists who claim that children should start their gardens from scratch, like true pioneers on virgin land; if so, they must be told by someone who calls a spade a spade that that sort of thing won't wash, for the children, with more choice that the backwoodsmen, would pull out before their backs and spirits were broken.)

79

Given an autumn garden, the children should be allowed to alter its design to suit themselves, but it should be face-lifted and planted up (with the plants and bulbs of their choice) by the beginning of November. Then they can forget all about it during the cold months until early spring brings the garden — and the children — to renewed crocus-bright life.

Seed Saving

Seed-saving on the allotment is always a gamble and may prove to be false economy, but who can deny the adventure of it? I usually allow a few specimens among my crops to live out their life span and run to seed if they so wish. Radishes, after a starry white flowering, produce fat seed pods; the smallest lettuces bolt into tall seedy elegance; brassicas bloom in a cloud of yellow glory; and a surviving salsify root can produce a handsome blossoming and seeding bush the following year.

An 18-month-old cabbage on my plot now looks as fresh as a daisy and has a chest measurement of 34 3/4 in. (88cm); a strongly staked and heavily seeding swiss chard (seakale beet) in its second year is all of six feet tall; and several of last year's parsnips, left in the ground through the winter, are now a yard high and umbelliforous with ripened sepia-brown seed heads that would comfortably supply all my plot neighbours.

Indeed, an inquiring young plot holder eagerly accepted a handful, apparently heedless, as he hurried away, of my warning that I couldn't guarantee the seed. Which leads me to wonder if allotment societies, inspired say by a member with expert knowledge of seeding processes and an awareness of the dangers involved, could not help with some organised seed saving. Perhaps some already do this; or are seriously exploring its possibilities and snags.

Last year my few young rhubarb plants, grown from seed which ripened in July, were later cut down by a dutch hoe, aggressively aimed at some cheeky enveloping chickweed. Misfortune also befell other gathered seeds, wrapped loosely in newspaper to dry, and absentmindedly left on the allotment in the mice-tenanted shed during the winter.

A seeding leaf beet left out in the cold, however, scorned my neglect to present me in early spring with a

81

clutch of young seedlings on its home ground (rather as a duck proudly presents her circle of downy ducklings). These quickly matured to provide us with a regular supply of spinach beet. What's more, they promise to do so for the future — which suggests an alternative gardening method, truly worthy of being called leisure gardening. By this method, you would lease for a few years a small patch of land to any willing vegetable and, so to speak, let it get on with it. Thinning and weeding would suffice — with an occasional application of fertiliser for good behaviour. Perhaps the leaf beets, root beets, and even carrots and parsleys would respond.

For me a gratifying success came this year with last year's saved peas (Carouby de Maussane, tall sugar; and Alderman) and beans (broad longpod and runner). On these I lavished especial care, keeping them cool, dry, darkish, and frost-free at home, and sowing them for a head start in early March in seed compost in a warm light porch. They germinated well. The sugar peas I planted out and staked, but they remained at a standstill for a period of cold weather. Even when three feet tall they gave no sign of blossoming. I was on the point of declaring them "blind" and tearing them ill-temperedly up when, with the blessed onset of better weather, they suddenly flowered in profusion and never looked back. Daily picking of the large flat "mangetout" pods provided us and friends with tasty helpings for six weeks or more. The elegant and full-podded Alderman also obliged.

What to do with unused packeted seed is a problem difficult to solve. Gone are the days when we on the allotments could afford to throw away the lot and start afresh. For my part, finding it almost impossible to throw anything away, I fold back the opened ends of the packets and store them in a narrow drawer, arranged alphabetically. I have a great number. A few have hieroglyphics such as "2d" on the packets.

Since some seeds, like radishes, lettuce, and beetroot, last several years — cabbage and marrow considerably longer — there seems to be some point in saving them, if only as a reserve to fall riskily back on. The one exception, all the experts agree, is parsnip seed, which cannot be kept at all. It is with considerable embarrassment therefore that I divulge what follows. I sowed some three-year-old Tender and True (Suttons) parsnip seed this year. I sowed it thickly, in early June, from an opened half-ounce foil packet, folded shut. And every time I look at this row of healthy parsnip plants my astonishment and ultimate delight go undiminished.

Further possible economies may be made at sales of surplus stock. Our local Co-op sells off, at vastly reduced prices, the packets of a well-known seed firm whose guarantee of viability ended in June.

Rubbish Recycled

Every decaying cabbage leaf or other piece of garden rubbish left lying about in winter, is a potential abode where a sly slug could set up home and eventually beget a large family. A slug, they say, lays about fifty eggs, and these can hatch out in the cosy warmth of rotting vegetable matter.

Traditionally rubbish suggests bonfires, though now that we are becoming aware of their nuisance value and the pollution involved, we should be actively discouraging the practice. The alternative — apart from the occasional tiny conflagration to deal with diseased growth, or with the root systems of couch grass — is composting.

On our allotment site the composters usually start with a rectangular base and four stout corner posts round which wire netting is fixed. One of our number recommends the digging of a preliminary pit covered by a grating of hedge prunings or strong stalks to separate the heap above from the air-pocket below. Both air and moisture are needed to promote the necessary bacterial activity. With too much water the process of decomposition is decelerated, but with shelter from cold winds and excessive rain, together with the use of "activators" you can speed it up.

The *Gardener's Companion and Diary* (published by the National Allotments Society) advises you to dig a shallow pit about a foot deep and fill it with ash, cinders, old mortar or fresh lime, mixed with a little soil and rammed down. The heap is built on this, layer by layer, soaked occasionally with any liquid manure, or with sulphate of ammonia water in, and given an occasional dusting of lime. After two months, the heap is turned completely over, and soon afterwards you should, with luck, possess some good, dark, crumbly manure.

The Royal Horticultural Society's publication, *The Vegetable Garden Displayed* (another best buy) advises a level base 9ft. by 4ft. on which to place and tread down your rubbish, followed by a layer of farmyard manure. Failing manure, sprinkle 2oz. of sulphate of ammonia over the rubbish and water the heap with 8 gallons of water. Over this put about an inch of soil.

As rubbish becomes available, repeat this process, and then apply ground chalk or limestone, followed by another watering and layer of soil. If and when the heap reaches a height of four feet, it is better to start another one. In dry weather you should water it every week, and you should turn the heap right over after a month in summer time, or six weeks in cooler seasons.

The Henry Doubleday Research Association, issues a valuable free leaflet on making compost and leaf mould. It explains how you can build a semi-detached wooden compost box, with one heap in the making and the other maturing; or you can drive into the ground, in a sheltered place, stout corner posts to a height of three feet on a four-foot square, and fix 2-inch mesh wire netting on both the inside and the outside of the posts to make a kind of cavity wall. Inside this cavity you stuff opened-up newspapers or cartons which will eventually rot, but will in the meantime enclose your rubbish and keep in the heat.

The argument is that if you can raise enough heat, by shelter and activators, you will kill off all weed seeds and send all pests to perdition. You should contrive to let air in at the bottom.

Theoretically anything that once had life — that is organic — can be put on your compost heap, though kitchen wastes are best in the middle of the heap and hard stalks should be chopped up. Things not to be overlooked are grass mowings, tea leaves, egg shells, cotton, wool or linen rags, and vacuum cleaner gleanings.

Equally important, however, are the things to keep out, like milk bottle tops, broken china, rose prunings, and plastics.

Carry on Mulching

My experimental year of no-digging and much-mulching on the allotment has now ended. It was not wholly successful. I shall therefore revert forthwith to the time-honoured custom of general digging. A light sandy soil, I guess, would not object to going undug, but my rather clayey loam had the appearance of suffering deprivation and neglect.

Much-mulching, however, cannot be faulted. It was the no-dig that failed for me. The main advantage was the inability to produce a fine tilth for seed sowing, so that my style of gardening had to change to sowing seeds in trays and blocks at home for planting out on the plot, with more rather than less labour involved.

I shall return to basic digging, but in a controlled way — not injurious, perhaps even beneficial — to pensioners like myself doing a small stint at a time as crops are cleared, using a light skinless steel spade, working only in suitable weather conditions, wearing comfortable loose clothing, and taking smaller than average spade bites to avoid back strain.

While turning over the soil, I shall turn over in my mind ways of improving and feeding the land. Drainage is all-important but not a serious problem for us because our plots are on a gentle north-south slope with a deep ditch at the southern end (into which I once backed my veteran Morris Minor — I had to be rescued by Pip, the market gardener over the hedge, who came to my aid with a tractor). Nevertheless, I shall contribute to our drainage by edging my plot and all its paths with distinctly dug-out gutterings, which, incidentally, will give the neat shipshape appearance much beloved by Nelson, my current *hors de combat* accomplice.

A farmer friend will again, I hope, provide me with a heap of well-rotted manure which I shall cover for protection through the winter to use next year for potato planting and soft fruit mulching. Other mulches — in my case, bark chips, grassmowings, and leaf mould (from home) — I shall use again to suppress weeds under and around all the soft fruit canes, cordons, and bushes. Growmore will be at hand to boost brassicas; fish, blood and bone, and calcified seaweed to encourage other crops. My next-plot neighbour sows mustard in September to dig in as green manure in spring.

Some of our plot-holders garden on the deep-bed system, bringing pieces of old carpet and lengths of black polythene into service for weed suppression, influenced perhaps by television programmes. We now have a friendly and horticulturally inventive woman who has turned her plot into a dozen or so small beds separated by a network of paths. She can sometimes be seen in a devotional attitude, on her knees at a bed-side, studiously hand-weeding or planting or placing old sheets of the *Guardian* securely over the paths to stem weed growth.

The vegetables and flowers on our plots seem to have liked this sometimes miserable summer. My peas, runner beans, and sweet pea flowers have been my best crops, but for these I had dug trenches last autumn. Unwin's First Early Onions and Giant Fen Globe — grown from sets in ground not specially prepared but which once had a manure heap on the site — have produced heavy crops to match those of my younger plot neighbours who always dig over their allotments, sometimes deeply, and if possible before Christmas and the January frosts.

Other good crops are courgettes and marrows, planted with liberal amounts of organic manure, and six Sigmabush outdoor tomatoes planted in a sheltered place, bearing a multitude of golf ball-sized fruit and waiting for an Indian summer to speed up ripening. Failing this, I must string up the laden clusters in the shed to ripen at leisure, or enclose some in drawers and be watchful.

But it is my new herb-collection-in-the-making that gives me most pleasure. Being largely untutored herb-wise but incurably experimental, I have been picking leaves, sprigs, and stems daily before they flower, popping them with all speed into freezer bags and the freezer, hoping they will lose none of their flavour and keep fresh until required.

From time to time I check with Elizabeth Cullum's *A Cottage Herbal* to see if I am on the right track in hanging small bunches upside down and, when dry after a week or two, removing the stems and powdering the leaves to keep in closed jars. For herb seeds (coriander; cumin, dill, and fennel) it is necessary to have sheets of paper to catch them as they fall from the bunches.

One day, perhaps, I shall aspire to making cheese and sage pie, thyme, cheese and tomato flan, sorrel soup, dill sauce, and many herb butters. Lacking that Indian summer, however, I must concentrate in the days ahead on the production of consignments of green tomato chutney.

With bonfire time approaching, it behoves us to beware of creating smoke nuisances; to burn for preference only diseased material and perennial weeds in small amounts; not to burn at night or in a strong wind; and to dig in the ash within a day or so to get any benefit from it.

Dutch Light

Sometimes on the allotment I think of the Dutch and submit to their teaching; because in affairs of the vegetable garden they seem to have an edge on us, making an art of simplicity. Look at any painting of a Dutch interior and you can tell there is a trim back-yard plot trying to get in.

Which is not to say that any good British allotmenteer is not as good as a Dutch counterpart. On both sides of the North Sea our allotments and gardens are subjected to the nuisance of cold winds and too much wet. In both countries we know equally well (not to get too scientific about it) that plants need food, warmth, air, and moisture; that Nature provides some of these requirements some of time and that we must do the rest. We know that beyond the spade and the fork nothing else is essential, unless perhaps a stout heart, a Dutch hoe and an English rake. But in two respects it seems to me, the Dutch are the experts: land-drainage and artificial warmth. So I think of the Dutch when I attend to my allotment drainage and when I wish I had some glass.

My plot is a level rectangle criss-crossed by seven grass paths to divide it into mini-plots. I always lift the soil away from the path edges — diking, as you might say — leaving gutters to drain off any surplus rainfall. And certainly my allotment never seems to look sodden and unkind.

As regards artificial warmth, Peter Shepheard says in his book *Gardens* that shutting out the wind from a plot of ground has the same effect as moving it 500 miles to the south. I can well believe it. Cold blasts out of Siberia sometimes sweep over our allotment and there is not a lot we can do about it; though a mixed foursome of new tenants – people in their prime – strongly fenced the north-east of their plot last year and made a patio on which they were enviously seen reclining in deck chairs and drinking cups of tea.

My market-gardening neighbour over the hawthorn hedge makes great use of Dutch lights. I look with admiration at the variety of constructional shapes and sizes: tall glass houses and low frames; long and short, wide and narrow, aesthetically pleasing and commercially productive. The Dutch light is surely an example of genius in simplicity. It is about 5ft. by 2ft. 6in.; a double-square and a constructional unit you can play with. But it never occurred to me that it might have a place on a small allotment until my market-gardening neighbour offered to let me have a few second-hand, "for the price of the glass". The offer was as welcome as it was unexpected, reducing it as the problem of expense and delivery of negligible proportions.

I said I would paint them white but this he discouraged. Anyhow, I could have cedar-wood frames if I wished. In fact he would be glad to get rid of them (made in the South, morticed at corners, liable to crack the glass if you were foolish to raise them at a corner). "Always use two hands" was his valuable advice, given free with the sale.

So now my head is buzzing with ideas for assembling my Dutch lights. Four stood on their sides and hooked or clamped at the corners, with two resting on the top, would make a deep "access frame" to give the lettuces a spurt or bring a blush of joy to an outdoor tomato; or one light with four short legs — a kind of low glass table — might cheer some chilled seedlings; or two leaning in a roof-shape (fastened by hooks or clamps) might make a gargantuan cloche to bring on the beans. The possibilities are endless. I might even — given time — emulate our leisure-gardening newcomers with a five-foot-tall glass fence to the north-east; or I might take it all round the plot, enclosing myself in an ivory tower of Dutch lights to grow peaches and pomegranates.

All I need now is a bit of Dutch courage.

Weeding for the Weak-kneed

Weeds are plants in the wrong place — unwanted, aggressively healthy and seemingly capable of withstanding flood, drought, and decimation. The weeds on my allotment, for instance, never look weedy, never lose heart or the lust for life. Observed dispassionately, they are often handsome plants. No disease ever seems to strike them. They flourish against all odds with a splendid resilience of spirit. It seems a pity that I cannot negotiate a treaty of friendship and non-aggression with them.

As things are, weed-suppression is a never-ending job. On my plot grass is the most persistent weed, and is two sorts, civilised and barbaric. The first is easily lifted by hand when the soil is moist (my wife's favourite job). The second — the hated couch grass and all its relations — I attend to myself, following them up with a fork to the farthest and deepest ramifications of their root systems; once out, I try never to take my eyes off them until they are destroyed. A hot sun will dehydrate them, a hard frost freeze them; but burning is best.

Similar incendiary treatment is wise for creeping buttercup, nettles, and ground-elder — not to mention the rampaging mint. You put these roots on your compost heap at your peril.

After the grasses, for pestilential persistence, come the cheeky and ubiquitous annual weeds - chickweed, fat-hen, groundsel, and the like. These may be attacked in various ways — with pull-hoe or dutch-hoe, by hand-fork or trowel; or, if you are a medievalist, with a widdick, weedock, or weedhook. But it is often pleasanter to pull them out by hand, especially after rain. The perennial docks and thistles, however, need special attention. Incorrectly confronted, they snap off at mid-root and grow again, several-fold.

These you must go for with a spade. A fork cannot cope because no matter how deep you go, the long tap-roots will elude the tines.

I have an admirable allotment neighbour whom I have never heard to swear. He has been weeding his plot joyfully, diligently, and continuously for months — ever since he took it over last year. It was overrun by couch grass and docks, which he has been steadily forking out and slow-burning on a bonfire that emits a thin wisp of smoke heavenwards for days on end. (He also turns up interesting grubs and larvae, which he can name.) By the time he has worked through the plot he has to begin again because perky green spikes have appeared once more. But his unremitting toil will triumph in the end.

I say this with confidence, remembering my own initial weed war, in the company of larks and a robin, week after toilsome week. And though I say it with fork and spade crossed, and fingers too, my plot is now reasonably clean and clear of weeds. Old Bob, our allotment mentor, encourages this fearless down-to-earth attack. He will have nothing to do with herbicides, believing them to be at best a cheat and at worst a poison. Hand and fork weeding is the only way to get an allotment clean, he maintains. That way, the plot belongs to you, not to invading bandits.

Of course some people haven't the time for this menial labour; or perhaps they don't like getting their nails dirty. But anyone who has once discovered the relaxations of garden-weeding will find the time and buy the gardening gloves. Because weeding really is — whether for reasons simple or psychologically complex — a wholesome and satisfying activity. It lifts the spirit and frees the mind.

"Good weeding!" one feels, should be the hearty salutation — the brightly exchanged greeting — of gardeners and allotmenteers everywhere as they look forward to therapeutically thumbing out blue birdseye and golden buttercups from among the beans, the beet and the broccoli.

Getting to Grips with the Mole

A gardener's enemies may be grouped into insect, bird, and four-footed foes; and since they are so much with us, it is useful to learn how to deal with, or put up with, them. For this reason, I give myself the occasional revisionary crash course.

To begin with the four-footed, and first, the mole — the genuine *Talpa europaea* — which, to its credit, consumes some larvae and slugs, but unfortunately much prefers our friendly earthworms, and recklessly undermines our crops in pursuit of them, or in searching for a mate.

He is a very active little beast, working, it is said, four-and-a half-hour shifts, with three-and-a-half hours off. He breeds till June. He hears extremely well, is sensitive to touch and smell, but sees little. If he undermines your vegetables and landscapes your garden with chains of hills, you can try to catch him with a Duffus, Pincer, or Fenn Trap, or you can look for a mole catcher to do it for you. Some local pest officers are willing to give demonstrations in setting mole traps, and local Ministry of Agriculture offices will supply names of people who deal professionally not only with moles, but with rats, mice, pigeons, rabbits, and other pests.

Only once did I have moles landscaping my own plot. I pushed pieces of thick and thorny bramble stems down into the runs — and the moles left. I have often wondered if they had already made plans to leave, or if they found the prickliness unpleasant. Some people advocate bottles, with open necks uppermost, pushed into the runs, so that the wind whistles down the bottle and perplexes the mole. Caper spurge bushes are said to deter them, on account of the poisonous sap in the stems. One of our plot-holders was a convert to this belief until he found his resident moles playfully making rings of molehills round the bushes.

Rabbits are becoming ever more troublesome on our plots, making us protect our winter greens with netting. We also have to discourage their nesting habits under huts and in the sides of rubbish heaps. They have in recent years acquired a taste for leeks.

A member of the Henry Doubleday Research Association living in the Yorkshire Pennines told how he successfully discouraged all rabbits by keeping a pet weasel in a cage at the top of his garden. On our allotments we have been accustomed to having a man with a gun and the shooting rights to hit the rabbits and miss the plot holders. Sunrise, when many rabbits and few humans are about, is a good time for this. If the man has a ferret as well as a gun, so much the worse for the rabbits. Gassing is something we don't like to think about, though the farmers have to adopt these drastic measures. Some of our people surround vulnerable crops like peas with string soaked in creosote to repel rabbits; and they put holly leaves or prickly furze twigs in seed drills to deter marauding mice.

Of the birds, pigeons with their large appetites can become a menace. Audible and visual scarers are some help, and the old fashioned scarecrow will not be scoffed at by birds so long as you remember to change its position from time to time, to give it a semblance of life and mobility. Bullfinches, it has been said, can be driven from the fruit beds by bits of strongly smelling onions hanging from the branches. Other small birds can be bothered by mock hawks, silver streamers, and floating balloons.

My own hostility, however, is more often directed at the insect world, at all those weevils, mites, aphids, moths, flies and midges; at those bugs, grubs and slugs; those miners, thrips, blights, wireworms and woodlice; those maggots and millipedes. Not forgetting the late summer harassment of wasps, nor the activities of flea beetles, leatherjackets and cutworms. More and more insecticides become available to gardeners obliged to confront these.

When cutworms bothered us badly at one time on our patch, my plot associate Nelson used a broken billiard cue and keen eye to prod those lurking miscreants to the surface and slay them. He always knew where to find them — round the stems of young cabbage plant, waiting for darkness to fall.

To withstand all these hostile competitors for our garden produce, we require resolution, and this is perhaps the time to resolve to be resolute. There are Ministry of Agriculture leaflets — single ones are supplied free — and the following may help: The Mole (No. 318), the Wild Rabbit (534), The Feral Pigeon (601), The Wood Pigeon (165), Wasps (GD35), Wireworms (199), Slugs and Snails (115), The Bullfinch (234).

Soft Fruit and Feathered Friends

My allotment is now restocked with strawberries — "Red Gauntlet" for romance and "Grandee" for size; and with raspberries — "Lloyd George" to honour the past and "Malling Jewel" to keep up with the present. I have also planted a thornless blackberry. All these are occasionally dressed with general fertiliser or mulched after rain with leaf compost. The strawberries are defended by thin scatterings of slug bait, the raspberries sprayed with lime-sulphur against cane-spot and with derris against the raspberry beetle. All I ask in return is a taste of home-made raspberry tart, a bowl of cool strawberries and cream and a glass of blackberry wine. But everything depends on the birds.

I like allotment birds. My favourites are the chorusing larks of early spring, the thrush that nests in a gooseberry bush, and the robin that rarely leaves me for most of the year. Nonetheless, when the soft fruits ripen, relations between us do become strained. At such times, I try to induce a mood of bird-orientated reasonableness, saying to myself "Birds are benefactors" and pondering on those pests — the saw-fly, greenfly, currant aphid, magpie-moth, red-legged garden weevil et al — which the small birds fall upon and devour with such fervour.

In this frame of mind I can mentally improvise harmless protective methods against our feathered friends. Lacking Victorian lace curtains I can for instance, thread the currant bushes with black nylon. For the strawberries and raspberries I envisage a display of tethered toy balloons above the fruit, and whirring toy windmills on sticks among the canes below.

Members of the Henry Doubleday Research Association have pooled other suggestions — from the breeding of real hovering hawks to the invention of artificial ones. Remembering how once I saw a tethered lighter-than-air red balloon floating in the breeze above an acre of crop and casting a dark moving shadow on the ground (with the consequence that not a single bird was in sight), it seems to me that the "hovering hawk" notion is worthy of development. Two feathers stuck in a potato suspended between two tall poles make a passable mock hawk, though a foot length of wood struck with long and short feathers will make a better one.

Other suggested bird-scaring devices are hanging bottles painted red, old electric bulbs, strips of tinfoil, dangling pieces of plain glass, models of cats' heads with evilly glinting glass eyes, flashing lights, and flying kites.

On my own patch, last year, I made a scarecrow out of old gardening clothes and rang the changes, having it one day leaning on a rake, the next appearing to wave a stick in the air, and so on, thus deluding a few of the birds for some of the time. More often, I fear, I deluded myself — whenever I caught sight of it out of a corner of my eye — into thinking that an unheralded visitor had appeared suddenly on the scene. And people going by deceived by the familiar old clothes and had, more than once passed the time of day to it.

Nelson Puts a Good Eye to the Glass

There are pros and cons for having a greenhouse on an allotment. The cons probably have it. Apart from not being able to give it the care and attention that you could devote to one at your back door, there are the other hazards and hindrances.

On our plot we do have a plastic-covered small one which is long past its prime. Indeed, it would have succumbed long since had not Nelson, my plot associate, used his improvisational skills to keep it on its feet and hold it steady with a piece of tough trawl net slung over and weighted down with bricks at the corners.

I have often wondered if we ought to be ashamed of our plastic greenhouse and have several times suggested to Nelson that we should replace it with a glossy glass and aluminium one. He says no. This one does us nicely, he says, and grows us more tomatoes than we need. It is at this point that I feel I have insulted his genius for improvisation and repair.

For recently we suffered a particularly tempestuous storm, and after an especially fierce howl and shriek of the blast, the greenhouses of our neighbours were suddenly brought low, flattened under twisted metal and flying glass. Our own — remarkably — remained unscathed, a monument to Nelson's genius for preservation.

For those unfortunates who are now having to replace shattered greenhouses, the Ministry of Agriculture has helpful leaflets for the asking. These are for commercial growers, of course, but we small fry can always pick up tips. The leaflet STL 28 (Glasshouse construction — siting and design) stresses the importance of avoiding the shade of buildings and trees, choosing a level site, avoiding heavy soil, ensuring good drainage, and seeking shelter against strong winds. The Booklet 2284 (Windbreaks for Glasshouses and Plastic Structures) discusses the effect of wind, and the cost, types, and relative effects of windbreaks, natural and artificial. Heat loss, it seems, doubles as wind speed increases from 0 to 15 mph. Leaflet 754 deals with, and is named, Strengthening Plastic-covered Structures Against Gale Damage.

On allotments, cloches are likely to be a better bet. Some of our plot-holders make their own, stretching polythene over wooden frames. Eric, our young enthusiast with experimental ideas and a productive plot, was given some discarded wire tree protectors. These, he found, he could shape to form pea guards or cover with plastic to make cloches. Glass or plastic sheets and strong wire are the essential. Plastic tunnels for rows of small seedlings and plants are not too difficult if you use pieces of bent wire both under the plastic to hold it up and over to peg it down.

Some years ago, my friendly market gardener over the hedge wished on me some cedar-framed dutch lights for which he had no further use. These were rather heavy and unwieldy and were passed on with instructions always and without exception to use both hands to move them. I found that four of them, stood on their sides, and hooked or clamped at the corners, with two on top, would make a deep access frame. Two lights, leaning together to make a roof shape,, or a single one as a lean-to against a wall or shed, could also prove useful if properly secured.

The *Gardening Which?* magazine gave valuable advice on cloches and plastic tunnels, with diagrams of the various types, results of tests on about 30 different makes and — perhaps of most use to economically minded plot holders — hints on making your own.

At the Northern Horticultural Society's Harrogate Harlow Car Gardens, where strong winds are a problem, they have grown attractive tall hedges as natural wind breaks. The model allotment they fenced on the windward side with Paraweb, an artificial wind break.

Clearing Winter Cupboards

A hibernating allotment is not without allure. It has more to offer than the last of the brussels sprouts, the first of the purple sprouting broccoli, and the main-crop leeks. Peace is all pervasive; no birds sing; and even the slugs — one suspects — are sleeping.

Still small voices, however, are calling you to off-season jobs; those crowns of rhubarb coming up through the path might be removed, the path edges trimmed, the rotting cabbage leaves gathered up, the diseased pea-sticks burned, the blackberry briars cut back and tied to the trellis, those premature blades of couch grass under the gooseberry bushes grubbed out.

As you move noiselessly about with bated, misty breath, the bare and slumbering earth reveals its own surprises: geologically interesting stones weathered to the surface during the winter; a rusty pocket knife; part of a suspender; a Biro pen; and plastic labels marked "Noel Sutton," "Air Warden" and "Queen Elizabeth."

And then you come suddenly face to face with a lost object, unexpectedly retrieved: that trowel which disappeared last autumn in mysterious circumstances while you were actually using it — and which, incidentally, you had supposed to be rustless — and that coin, last remembered loose in a pocket with bits of garden string but missing when fumbled for to pay for spring cabbage plants in the village shop.

A sleeping allotment also floods the mind with ideas for developing one's domain. That old garden frame, for instance, probably Georgian in origin and now incapable of further preservation — reluctantly, it must go. And the toolshed, formerly a Victorian chicken-house, with a long history of humble, creosoted service; and the grass paths, some of which are certainly an extravagance — these too must go.

The turves can be used as bricks to wall in the compost corner. Certain features, however, must be preserved: that crescent-shaped flower bed, for one, where giant sunflowers last year grew tall enough not only to conceal the toolshed but to laugh at the tower blocks on the distant horizon. This year the bed shall have Indian corn, or Jerusalem artichokes perhaps, to make a landscaping feature.

It is the day the farmyard manure is delivered that puts an end to this pleasant winter planning and pottering. I had always supposed genuine farmyard manure to be no longer obtainable, but this is not so. It lies like Himalayan foothills about our allotments, arriving by the double-load for economy of transport. It is dumped on the public track at the end of the plot, holding up all traffic till it is removed. It assails the nose and offends the eye. But who could complain about this high pile of treasure — this horticultural gold? With a wheelbarrow before me and head held high, I go forward into the busy season.

The Worm
and the Earth

Red in Tooth and Claw

An allotment is not continuously a place of calm contemplation and quiet creativity — not even in a gentle rural setting where birds sing and bees drone.

Take, for instance, the hare. It was in the fallow days of February, on visiting my new piece of land, that I startled a hare out of a blackberry thicket at the end of the plot, near the hawthorn hedge and the market garden. It had presumably set up home there, and had probably gone undisturbed throughout the weeks of winter. I can still see its startled eyes and alertly erect ears as it darted through the hedge and ran its own Olympic across the market-gardener's spring cabbages. "I shall never see it again," I thought, ruefully, as it faded into the rainbow light of the sunset.

But one day in summer, the crack of a shotgun over the hedge was followed by the sight of the market-gardener holding up by its hind legs a very long and lifeless-looking hare. "Eating my lettuces," he explained.

Then there was the mole. Not everyone has seen a molehill in the making. I watched the mounds rise out of the fallow ground of my domain, as islands sometimes rise out of the sea. The earth churned mysteriously, coming up like minced meat. "Well done, old mole," one murmured. One admired him, for his power to move mountains.

Well that was back in February, before the plot had been reclaimed from the ravages of rampaging nature. Now, it is a different story. The other day, for instance, my neat rows of kale and broccoli were undermined before my very eyes. Only by a supreme effort of will could I stay my own hand from grabbing a long-pronged fork from the hut, to attack that newly formed Pennine Chain of rounded hills. As it is, the mole remains, and earth movements are endemic; so far, however, the brassicas appear not to be too disturbed, either by the earth-shaking or by the scenic changes to their immediate environment.

Then there were the birds. At first, one bird alone appeared to be resident on the plot — a robin. He proved a close and constant companion during weeks of clearing, digging and planting. Then — sadly — he went; just about the time when visiting and less welcome birds were arriving without stint. St Francis never had so many birds to talk to as I had at the height of the soft-fruit season.

There was the thrush that settled on top of a beanpole to dazzle my wife and me with full-throated song before diving to steal a strawberry. Then there were the smaller birds that came in swarms to creep under the fruit nets and enjoy themselves at their leisure, heedless of our cries of "shoo." At such times savage thoughts and unruly passions had to be suppressed.

But the problem of the birds was as nothing to the problem — indeed the mystery — surrounding half a dozen genuine birds nests, bequeathed to us in a box the allotment hut. This hut contained, when we took over, an interesting assortment of horticultural items. There was a half-used packet of peas, a box of soot, some lengths of border-twine, a plastic fruit net, and this cardboard box labelled "fruit salads" but containing genuine birds' nests.

When I first saw these nests, I imagined that an earlier tenant had taken them in from the hedge, out of the rain, to store them through the winter. This may, in fact, have been the case; but after those depredations by our feathered filchers among the fruit, I took a more jaundiced view. It seemed more likely that the nests had been confiscated though not barbarously destroyed.

Somewhat guiltily, I took the nests from the box and lodged them without delay between suitable forked branches of the hawthorn hedge. And within a week, yellow-hammers were nesting.

Dare one hope that the robin — once so attached to us but now missing for so long — might one day return with a bride to occupy another part of our (or his?) ornithological real estate?

The Worm Turns

I told before how Nelson, my gardening associate, introduced a fugitive family of hedgehogs to our allotment. Hedgehogs are free ranging, but I hoped they might settle with us and enjoy our slugs. A lady from Buckinghamshire wrote to say that milk was wrong for them so I contacted the British Hedgehog Preservation Society without delay for advice.

Their helpful and sympathetic education officer, H.L.C. Sharp, referred me to the book *Hedgehogs,* by Pat Horns of the Zoology Department, London University, published by Whittet Books. Dr Morris says an exclusive diet of bread and milk to young captive hedgehogs could be harmful because they need more variety. Their natural food consists of beetles, caterpillars, earthworms, and to a lesser extent slugs, snails, millipedes, earwigs, and larvae, all of which they will usually find in relative abundance on our allotment; though as gardeners we cannot wholly approve their liking for that valuable gardeners' friend, the earthworm.

It is a good idea occasionally to check up on our garden wildlife friends and helpers so as to be able to protect and encourage them. In the case of the deserving hedgehog, we can provide suitable places (dry leaves, space under sheds) for it to nest; and we can make sure there isn't one resting under the rubbish heap before making a bonfire.

The true hedgehog fancier will be thinking just now of rescuing autumn orphans, keeping them warm with hay or newspaper in a box, feeding them on minced meat, scrambled egg, bread and bran, with a constant supply of fresh water, and releasing them one fine day to build a winter nest and hibernate.

An informative illustrated leaflet is published jointly by the British Hedgehog Preservation Society and the RSPCA.

To turn to the earthworm, equally deserving of praise and commendation. It helps to drain and aerate the soil, brings up mineral substances from deep down, improves the crumb structure of the top soil, and supplies it with wormcast compost. Charles Darwin in his book, *Vegetable Mould And Earthworms,* estimated that wormcasts are delivered in and on the soil at a rate of 10 tons per acre per annum and that across a span of years all the topsoil, passes through the bodies of worms, thus becoming enriched, and even limed by their calciferous glands.

Other garden helpers, when they have the luck to elude deadly chemical sprays, are birds, bees, ladybirds, hoverflies, lacewings, centipedes, ground beetles, and the attractively named devil's coach horse beetle. With these we should make an effort to familiarise ourselves. Publications like *Pest Control Without Poisons,* by Lawrence D. Hills of the Henry Doubleday Research Association, can help.

As for the hostile insects, on a small vegetable plot we can with some effort and agility learn to detect, capture, and summarily dispatch at least some of the flies, fleas, beetles, bugs, mites, moths, and maggots that we come across. Nelson can do this expertly. Me, I am always promising myself a preliminary home study course on insect pest detection.

Flea beetles and other leaf eaters have finally got at my chinese greens which were spared earlier on. However these pests were persuaded to leave by covering the greens with plastic netting.

Joy Larkcom (A Taste Of Taiwan, *RHS Magazine*) tells how the gardeners on that island use low nylon nets over their crops, both as a barrier to airborne insects, and a protection against wind and rain. She was greatly impressed by the Taiwanese gardeners, as I was by the Chinese gardeners of Hong Kong during a winter sojourn there in the early seventies.

I well remember a ferry trip to Lamma Island to admire extensive patchworks of vegetables in their terraced valley strips. A Chinese youth stopped to ask my wife and I if we were lost. Only in admiration, we told him, whereupon he invited us to his family's vegetable farm higher up the valley, worked by his mother and grandmother while he ferried daily to sell radios in Hong Kong. This vegetable farm was about the size of our allotment, but it had its own well, water pipes, and irrigation ditches with close vegetable patches at different stages of growth. They too had had their pests — blister beetles and sting bugs.

It was in Hong Kong at that time that I came across the work of G.A.C. Herklots who, during four years of internment by the Japanese, made a hillside garden and wrote a book about the vegetables he grew on it. Interesting therefore to learn that on her recent visit to Taiwan, Joy Larkcom's Research Director guide told her that his horticultural bible was the late Dr Herklot's *Vegetables in South-east Asia.* Those long years of internment had not been in vain.

Emulating Chinese neatness, I have cut out the old rasp canes on our plot and tied up the young ones. After reading the adulatory article, Autumn Fruiting Raspberries by David Parsons (also *RHS Magazine*), I am keen to introduce some myself. Though September is the well known variety he writes of an arrival from Switzerland, Zeva, and two from America, Fallgold (yellow) and Heritage, but above all East Malling's Autumn Bliss, said to be a good cropper and available shortly.

Also taking a tip from the Chinese, I have transplanted my spring cabbages (Spring Hero) more closely to give them the clustered companionship that should help them through the winter.

Family Friends

Back in March, as I was working on my allotment, an unusually large flock of starlings temporarily darkened our sky. The effect was quite disturbing, especially when lower echelons of birds broke away from the whirring mass to swoop low over our plots before hedgehopping away — a reminder of those swarms of locusts in foreign parts that descend and demolish fields of grain before you can say *shoo;* and I fell to thinking how tenuous is the shield that protects us gardeners from conceivable calamity.

Not that gardeners need fear starlings (unless they grow cherries). Farmers may be excused some apprehension, lest those myriads of migrating mouths should descend for a quick lunch from the feeding troughs and leave behind (as some say) fowl pest and foot-and-mouth. But we home gardeners and allotmenteers have good cause to befriend those few starlings who strut, confident and sure-footed, about our lawns and plots, determined on helping us get rid of our leather-jackets, click beetles, wireworms, and assorted larvae. Their beaks turn a welcoming spring-yellow to match the celandines.

We plot-holders are, in fact, rather slow to admit that we have friends as well as pests on our plots. We acknowledge the robins and ladybirds, or course, and there the list usually ends, but ask us to name our garden pests and we can rattle off a dozen or more without taking breath. The garden books are equally unfriendly in this respect, with one or two exceptions. *The Gardener's Assistant* (in six volumes) is one such exception. It actually has a chapter entitled Garden Friends.

First compiled in the last century by a superintendent of the RHS Gardens, it was revised, re-modelled, and re-published in 1925 by William Watson, a curator of Kew Gardens, and since that time has no doubt assisted many gardens. Watson mentions around fifty garden friends and

I have been trying to get acquainted with some of them on my allotment, magnifying glass in hand, and Collins's *Insect Field Guide* in my pocket.

It seems best to separate into two groups the creatures that by some kind of divine right inhabit and share our gardens. These are the herbivores and the carnivores — the vegetarian leaf eaters, and the meat eaters who eat them. Broadly speaking, the vegetarians are our enemies because they eat our vegetables, and the meat eaters are our friends because they eat the vegetarians. There is a third group, of course: the omnivores — our sometime friends, as when they devour the fruit pests, and sometime enemies when they go for the fruit itself.

Robins are both friends and partners; ladybirds are gentle creatures that make mincemeat of the greenfly on our roses. This friendly assistance must be acknowledged in passing, before going on to the beetles and birds that are also our benefactors. Take, for instance, the common Rove Beetle — or the Devil's Coach Horse Beetle to those who know no better than to demean it. (Nearly a thousand species, Collins say.) The Magnificent Rove Beetle, as I shall call it forthwith, may be identified as over an inch long, narrow for a beetle, with wings that are neatly tucked away when not in use, and with scorpion-like habits and demeanour. It is predacious, ferocious, and tenacious as a bull-dog.

Touch it with a stick and it will curl its tail over its head to fire volleys of venom at its supposed attacker. With its great jaws it can clip earwigs into pieces and devour the soft parts with the greatest of ease. (Dahlia growers, please note.) You can come upon it at any time except in May, when it is otherwise engaged, but it is around quite a lot in autumn. All told, therefore, you should regard the Magnificent Rove Beetle (at arm's length) as a friend and ally and never destroy it.

Then there is the Ground Beetle, which may be found lurking under stones and clods of earth. You identify it by the violet gloss on the edges of its shoulders, and grant it

111

instant reprieve. The glow-worm is another friend which I remember, as a boy, lighting up Oxfordshire hedge banks on dark or moonlit nights. It feeds on the soft centres of snails.

And to join the ladybirds in their good works, we have the hoverflies and the large-eyed, long-winged lacewings, whose larvae also devour aphids by the score. And what the ichunemon fly does to the caterpillars around is not pretty, but most helpful. Nor must we forget the humble earthworm, the greatest friend of all.

There are also three friendly carnivorous slugs, or slug-like snails, about three inches long, yellow and brown. They carry a half-inch long shell on the back, at the tail end. If recognised, they should be allowed to roam, which they do at night. Spiders are carnivorous too, and if you can excuse the webs you should adopt a let-live attitude towards them. And frogs, toads and lizards you should greet with a smile.

Among the birds I recognise the hedge sparrows and yellow hammers that nest in my hawthorn hedge as insect-eating friends, and I would welcome the cuckoo as a temporary lodger for the caterpillars that would thereby receive short shrift. Many of the larger birds live variously on leather jackets, wireworms, mice, voles, young rats, slugs, and snails, and thus contribute to the undercover reign of terror that keeps our gardens tranquil.

In the old days, I understand, gardeners used to tame amenable members of the crow family — jackdaws and choughs for instance — to have about the garden. They used to clip their wings to prevent them straying. Magpies, lapwings, and herring gulls used to be considered similarly tameable, and useful: their beaks are strong enough to pull out grubs near the surface. I must ask our old-time villagers about this. A re-introduction of such bird-help might be worth trying — unless the Bird Protection Act makes illegal the wing-cutting part of the process. I think I should like a jackdaw as an allotment pet.

112

Relying on a Bed of Nettles

After wintry weather throughout April, only now are Shakespeare's darling buds of May bravely but still cautiously burgeoning in our parts. Attempts at progress on the allotments have been mainly from the paths. Also, as in recent years, it has been wise to delay small seed sowing in the open. Those who go by the book have probably had their efforts go by the board as well.

Driven indoors by inclemency, I continued propagation thanks to the generous window space of my west-facing workroom and a well lit porch at the front — geranium (Cherry Diamond) and ornamental capsicum (Candlelight) from seed; Red Alert tomatoes for outdoors started in the airing cupboard and pricked out into individual pots after a few days; sweetcorn (Early Xtra) and courgettes (Ambassador). John Higgins, in an article on courgettes in the *RHS Journal*, considers Ambassador favourite among growers. A National Institute of Agricultural Botany trial of eight varieties found Ambassador to be early, dark green, narrow, and high yielding, averaging 22 per plant.

I also have some celeriac (Iram) hardening off to face the rigours of the allotment scene. Some years ago I tried sowing celeriac in the open with no success, apart from a rather pleasant celery-like smell emanating from the soil afterwards. This year, with my healthy looking celeriac plants in trays, I have high hopes of enhancing the home-made allotment soup on which I thrive. I make it in bulk, put it through a blender, and store it in both fridge and freezer. September is the time to harvest and store celeriac, though you can leave it in the ground so long as you provide some protection against hard frost.

We are devoting a third of our plot to flowers this year and reducing the ground given to potatoes which last year seem to have been the staple diet of slugs. We are concentrating on sweet peas for which manured trenches have long been prepared. My own Champagne Bubbles will vie with the 48 plants in eight varieties of Unwin's Histon Collection.

For the sake of the butterflies we are also allowing free rein to a small bed of nettles under the hawthorn hedge at the end of the plot. This will be our contribution to the current wildlife and wild garden movement. Vacant plots, of course, can quickly become wildlife sanctuaries in themselves. I well remember, back in the sixties when I took on such a wilderness, how I watched entranced as larks around me ascended, carrying their soaring song into sunlit May skies. We had more of them then — both neglected plots and jubilant larks.

A Harvest of Hedgehogs

A week or two ago my plot associate Nelson encountered six young hedgehogs leisurely passing our allotment. They were clearly departing their homestead to explore the wide world of slugs, snails, black millipedes etc. With great presence of mind and unhindered by the spines, Nelson deftly deposited them along our crops and did his best to make them feel welcome. The soil being dry, he sank a small trough of water in the ground to satisfy their thirst in case they failed to capture enough juicy slugs for this purpose.

In the event, the youngsters were quite nimble and adventurous. Being myself untutored in natural history but always willing to learn, I became a hedgehog watcher on the instant and fixed an inquisitive eye on one of them, never missing a move. Completely at ease, it nosed unhurriedly among the crops until finally it disappeared into the undergrowth of a neighbour's plot. As a family, these hedgehogs seem now to have dispersed and gone their separate ways, though we hope they will become anti-slug benefactors to the allotments generally.

With regard to our resident slugs, the monsters actually had a go at my first early potatoes. In consequence, I aim to dig up my main crop of King Edwards (a favourite of theirs, I believe) without delay in a determined attempt to thwart them.

Fortunately, apart from slugs, we quite noticeably have not been bothered (touch wood) by pests so far this season. At the moment (touch wood again) I cannot see a single flea beetle perforation in the leaves of my three varieties of young Chinese greens, which suggests there is wisdom in gathering the leaves while still young and unsullied. This I intend to do. I am already using the thinnings of leaf beet in this way, cutting off the roots and steaming the young stems and leaves together to make a tasty vegetable at table.

It has been a good year for lettuce too. Little Gem — a small cos with cabbage tendencies — has done me proud over past weeks, likewise the crispheads Lake Nyah and Lakeland.

To continue this strain of unbridled self-congratulation, we have had an excellent soft fruit harvest. My bushes and cordons certainly benefited from a generous mulch of farmyard manure earlier in the year. So far there is no sign of mildew among the gooseberries, nor of sawfly denudation. Nevertheless I am not so caught up in horticultural cloud-cuckoo-land as to be unready for some widespread hand-picking of caterpillars quite soon. After the fruit picking, this minor sport makes a change.

The Ministry of Agriculture, Food and Fisheries (MAFF) has leaflets on new varieties of strawberries, bush fruits and cane fruits (P930/1/2 respectively). These are aimed at commercial growers but are not without interest to the allotmenteer. Of the strawberries, Elvira is early, Hapil and Cambridge Favourite mid-season, and Bogota late. Of the new raspberries, East Malling's Joy and Leo (Lloyd George and Norfolk Giant among their forebears) as well as Scotland's Glen Moy and Glen Prosen, are commercially available. So is the blackberry Ashton Cross, which crops well and has a good flavour.

Among the newer hybrid berries are East Malling's sunberry, said to have a flavour which is sweet with a hint of blackberry, and Tayberry which has a season from early June to mid-August. Tummelberry is an offshoot of the Tayberry (just as the Tummel is a tributary of the Tay). Compared with Tayberry the fruits are shorter, the flavour sharper, the ripening a week earlier and the yield slightly lower. But Tummelberry is considered to be more hardy.

As for bush fruits, new varieties of blackcurrant are Scotland's Ben Lomond (large berries), Ben More (ripens earlier), Ben Nevis (yields well), and Ben Sarek (a small bush). Holland has Black Reward (consistent fruiting) and East Malling Jet (large and vigorous bush).

New gooseberries listed are East Mallings Greenfinch (Careless is a parent) and Invicta (heavy cropping). Both are said to be resistant to mildew.

MAFF also issues leaflets on cut flowers. These are of interest to allotmenteers like myself who, more and more, include flowers on their plots. They explain, for example, how to cut at the correct stage, and how to assist uptake of water in the stems; and they tell you to keep flowers away from ripening fruit because of ethylene emission.

Do You Know Your Enemies?

Except to gather winter greens, we do not often visit our winter allotments. Wild life reigns over them. The rodents, as is their custom, have taken up residence in and under the garden huts, and in this connection forewarned is forearmed.

Last year, Nelson, my plot associate, left a store of gathered vegetables for me to pick up in time for Christmas which, on account of the weather, I failed to do. A week later he found them all but demolished. The mice of all the neighbourhood, he suggested, had gathered in our shed for a midwinter feast. They had explored the hearts of the cabbages, shredded the onions, sorted out the beets, and peeled the parsnips. Moreover, at the end of last year's hard winter, either because of severe hunger or through exasperation at finding nothing better, they had chewed up left-behind clothes — caps, gloves, scarves — even old sacks and polythene bags.

Rabbits range and forage, but a rabbit in winter has a lean time on our plot. Our winter greens are well protected by wire and plastic netting of which Nelson has a useful store. Rabbits, however, are enterprising. They find ways under the netting to get at the brassicas or, with even more astuteness, seek out those plots whose owners have failed to protect their crops.

And no birds sing. The robin, however, still chirps at us, meets and greets us as we approach on our rare visits. He is rightly acknowledged to be the gardener's friend, though the gardener has other friends too, if less easily recognised; and it is as well to remind ourselves of these less obvious friends and helpers.

It is only too easy to regard with a general hostility the wild life that shares our gardens and co-tenants our plots. The old *Gardener's Assistant,* edited by William Watson, one-time curator at Kew, contains a lengthy list of would-be friends among the animals and insects that inhabit our gardens. All these, he says, sort themselves out into two groups, the carnivores and the herbivores — very few, like wasps and earwigs, are both. Our true enemies are the herbivores — the vegetarians who eat our crops. Our friends are the meat eaters who, with commendable carnivorous inclinations, devour our enemies, the vegetable eaters.

Those deep black, narrow bodies, and big headed scorpion-like Rove Beetles, for instance, prey fearlessly on earwigs and other insects. The glow-worm has predacious encounters with snails. Ladybirds have a praiseworthy appetite for aphids. Bees, apart from a possibly calyx-piercing proclivity among broad and runner beans, are an overall pollen-spreading good.

Birds can be useful if they are insectivorous or feed upon mice and voles. Always it is necessary to weigh up their benefactions against the harm they may do. Certainly, the soft fruit filchers can become deadly enemies in June and July to those gardeners lacking fruit cages. Buntings, however, are partly insectivorous during the summer. The yellow hammers that used to inhabit and enhance the hawthorn hedge at the end of our plot, were always easily exonerated. Alas, they are no longer with us. I would gladly surrender a fair share of raspberries to them if only they would return. The cuckoo, too, is now more rarely heard in our parts. Being insectivorous, it was a gardener's friends as well as the harbinger of our rural summer.

Finches are seed eaters. They feast themselves on neglected plots that have run to seed, and consequently help to stop the spread of weeds to other more civilised patches. They also enjoy caterpillars.

The crow family is largely beneficial too, feeding on cockchafer grubs, wireworms, leatherjackets, cutworms, slugs, and grubs. Gulls that come inland to follow the plough are a benefit to farmers. Black-headed gulls, lapwings, and magpies are said to be tameable if you take the initial and seemingly painless measure of cutting their wings.

And that's not the end of bird benefactions. Owl capture mice, partridges weevils, pheasants wireworms, poultry caterpillars and grubs, starlings leatherjackets, swallows and martins insects on the wing, thrushes slugs and snails.

Nelson has rapport with our own feathered friends, as you expect of a true countryman. Year by year, he guards and protects a linnet's nest in our gooseberry cordons. Once he became so well known to the bluetit fledglings (whose garden hut residence ensured them a happy childhood) that when they made their first hesitant flight, they landed on his shoulders.

Frogs and toads are innocent do-gooders in a garden. Hover flies should never be swatted. Genuine spiders are our friends.

In Praise of English Apples

Three cheers for English apples. The French may have their pears, the Italians their peaches, and more distant places their pomegranates and papayas, but allow us to glorify our apples and brag about them.

The apples in my garden that I see daily through my windows I care for the year round as I would a pet. They are indeed the apples of my eye. Others who live alone have their dogs, cats, and budgerigars; I have my apple cordons, now reaching or perhaps passing middle age. Over the years they have been allowed freedom to dip laterally, arch vertically over, entwine and embrace their neighbours, though they are subjected to discreet July and December pruning.

At one time they were given a winter tar oil wash and summer sprays against the capsid bug and coddling moth. Nowadays, as a reasonable alternative, I thin the fruit when green and thereafter feed and water well.

For as long as I can remember, the apple has had great significance in myth and legend. There was athletic Atalanta, for instance, who lost a race because she paused to pick up apples; and William Tell, who was compelled to shoot an apple off the top of his boy's head... thank heaven his aim was good. Then there was that American folk hero, Johnny Appleseed, living rough, sleeping with bears, penetrating the wilderness, scattering apple pips to give the frontiersmen a future of apple pie and strong cider.

It was while working briefly in the US — eating a large Mackintosh red daily for lunch, and missing my English apples — that I made an interesting discovery. The legendary Johnny Appleseed was, in fact, John Chapman (1774–1845) who paddled his canoe up creeks of the Ohio River with another canoe in tow laden with rotten apples to start his orchards.

A lover of nature from childhood, friend of Indians, to

whom he gave the seeds of healing herbs, his nomadic life was lived travelling from one young apple orchard to the next, co-operating with or combatting Nature as necessary, and willing to exchange an apple sapling for old clothes. He died an old man in Indiana, attending to the last his thriving orchards. A monument commemorates him there.

There must have been Johnny Appleseed on this side of the Atlantic, perhaps too modest to acquire renown. Certainly there have been poppers of pips in plant pots aplenty. (An allotment neighbour is one such with a nursery of young fruit trees at the end of his plot.)

Richard Cox produced the first Cox's Orange Pippin by happy chance near Slough; George Kempster, the Kempster (later Blenheim) Orange at Woodstock; Mary Ann Brailsford the original Bramley Seedling, now propped up but still producing when I last saw it behind a Nottinghamshire cottage. And there are other originals worthy of note. The Newton Wonder was found in a Derbyshire thatched roof, the Claygate Pearman in a Surrey hedge.

To consult the National Apple Register is fascinating. I have, for instance, a Ribston Pippin and learn about its ancestry. The original was raised in the park of Ribston Hall, North Yorkshire, from a pip — it must be admitted — that came like William the Conqueror from Normandy, c. 1709. The tree was blown over in 1810, but, supported on props, lingered another 30 years.

It was a pip of a Ribston Pippin that Richard Cox planted to get his Cox's Orange Pippin that conquered the world with its flavour. My two Cox's cordons do their ancestors less than justice, however, being too far north of Slough.

My Laxtons — Superb, Fortune and Epicure — all stem from crosses of Cox's Orange with other eating apples. They yield well, as do my Egremont Russet (of somewhat shrouded origin) and my James Grieve; derived from a seed of Pott's Seedling which, in turn, had two

American apples as parents.

Thomas Laxton — Victorian and handsome — was a famous plant breeder whose two sons, Edwards and William of Bedford, turned their energies to fruit hybridisation and trees in pots for the crossing of thousands of apples to produce a score or so of very successful named varieties.

Of the latest modern varieties I cannot speak, though I admired specimens of Discovery in the Vale of Evesham the other day. The *Gardening Which?* magazine recommended George Cave, Kaija, Sunset and Crispin, planted together to give apples from August to February.

Three additional cheers therefore for the professional pomologists who nowadays speak and work in terms of clones, chromosomes and columnar (single stem) trees, not forgetting the lucky amateurs like Brewer Cox with his Orange Pippin and Ms Brailsford with her Bramley Seedling — nor the committed orchardists like Johnny Appleseed.

Plant
Listing

A Ripe Time for Rejoicing

In mid-June on the allotment I observed my annual ritual. I dug up the first root of potatoes, hurried home, boiled them with a sprig of mint, ate them with melted butter, and rejoiced. There is nothing quite like your first boiling of new potatoes, provided they come fresh from your own garden, the product of your own gardening.

It is surprising how often modern technical advances and conveniences can spoil things. New potatoes from a foreign field can never taste as good. And last year's freezer-preserved gooseberries eaten up in May — with their flavour gone — can spoil your anticipation of the freshly-plucked berries from the bush in July.

It is the same with freshly-pulled young carrots, with crisp Little Gem lettuce, newly-picked heads of calabrese, and quickly-cooked portions of Swiss chard stems when given no time to dehydrate.

This is one important reason for growing your own fruit and vegetables and flowers for cutting. Some would say it is the most important reason.

Of course, the beneficial exercise, open air, freedom, and satisfactions of working productively on the soil are additional arguments for having a garden of your own. As far as cut flowers like sweet peas are concerned, it is clear that freshness is all important.

I mention sweet peas particularly because I am so pleased with my own. Nelson says I ought to show them at the village show this week but modesty, laziness, or fear of devastating defeat stays my hand. But certainly I have extended more care than usual to their cultivation.

Last autumn I dug their trench to receive kitchen waste and compostible material in modest amounts, with a little farmyard manure, after first forking loose the subsoil.

In January I sowed the seeds singly in small pots of Levington compost mixed with perlite. I germinated them

127

in the airing cupboard, removing them on emergence to a south-facing window to catch the gentle January-Febuary sunshine.

I pinched out the tops of the seedlings after the third leaf, and later chose the strongest of the shoots from the base to be the favoured cordon.

After hardening off gradually from indoor to outdoor conditions, I planted them in the trench in April, having earlier filled it in, broken down lumps, removed any infant weeds, and mixed in a little bone meal, calcified seaweed and superphosphate.

As the cordons grew, I fastened them to their tall canes with plant rings — raffia would be better, I think — and nipped out the side shoots and tendrils (now a daily task, as is the cutting of the blooms). As the flower buds developed, coinciding with a dry spell, I watered them well which they obviously appreciated.

The flower stalks, at present about 18in long, possess a commendable firmness and strength, usually with four blooms to a stalk. I fear I shall falter at the labour involved when the plants reach the top of their canes, expecting to he untied, trained alongside the row at ground level to start climbing a new cane.

I have 10 varieties, including Jilly (cream turning to ivory), Alastair (cherry red), and Cambridge Blue (frilly blooms and scented). Also from Unwins I have Diamond Wedding (white and scented), Hunter's Moon (deep cream and scented), Evensong (soft blue merging with lilac and scented), Sally Unwin (rose pink, shading to white and scented), Pink Bouquet (pink, salmon pink and white, scented), Fiona (salmon pink on cream, scented), Percy Thrower (light lilac on white, scented), and Rosy Frills (white ground, rose edge, scented).

Years ago when my wife was alive, she valued our allotment above all for the sweet peas, which she cut throughout the summer and arranged around the house. This summer I shall try to repeat the practice, marvelling at the charm and elegance of these present varieties and registering a silent thanks to those breeders and suppliers of modern strains.

Those of us who value our allotment plots will welcome the exhaustively researched and comprehensive allotment book by David Crouch and Colin Ward.*

The authors analyse the merits and demerits of the Thorpe Allotment Report, so painstakingly prepared and so unforgivably ignored by successive governments. The human element and mystique of plotholding is prominent in the book, in all the individualism, diversity, creative self-expression and innate attachment to the soil which it displays.

* *The Allotment: Its Landscape and Culture,* by David Crouch and Colin Ward (Five Leaves)

You Don't Have to Provide Umbrellas

Potatoes and rhubarb are happy enough on an allotment. So are gooseberries, which repay you well, even for a minimum of care bordering on neglect. They are rugged, resourceful and resilient. Local names like goosegogs and honeyblobs stem from the thorny hedgerows they used to inhabit, to be picked over for food by our fearless forbears.

The gooseberries on our own plot are over 20 years old and still going strong. Fifty years, I believe, is not impossible. For longevity, therefore, they have the advantage over other berried fruits. In 1821 it was claimed that a bush at Duffield in Derbyshire attained a circumference of 12 feet while another one, trained along a wall as a cordon near Chesterfield, achieved a 50ft length of growth.

On our plot we have half a dozen buxom bushes five feet apart, and a row of gooseberry cordons at 15in intervals. Additionally, I once grew — from cuttings which are easy — low gooseberry hedges along the boundaries of the plot to discourage aggressors and repel invaders. In those days the berries were gathered in sacks rather than baskets. The hedges harboured weeds, of course, like couch grass and bindweed; for this reason Nelson recommended, and promptly put into action, some gooseberry deforestation, so that the hedges are no more. Even so, we still have ample harvests of berries for pies, fools, sauces, chutneys, jams, jellies, wine, and gift givings.

The gooseberry therefore deserves some praise and commendation; and when, as we hope, those vicious thorns are eventually bred out of them, they will undoubtedly become popular. With cordons you can dodge the thorns more easily, and also with bushes if, wearing stout gloves, you open them up, thin out the branches, remove lower shoots and suckers, and give them a leg to stand on.

Lancastrians and other northern gooseberry fanciers also deserve commendation. Over the past couple of centuries, with their clubs, shows, and keen competition, they have exerted themselves to produce bigger berries. Some years ago, I remember visiting the gooseberry garden of enthusiastic Mr Ventriss in Egton near Whitby who provided his prize gooseberry bushes with umbrellas to protect them from excessive rain and the danger of splitting their sides.

The gooseberry plant seems to like Britain best and America hardly at all. Though rather late, ours crop well in their open, moist, but well drained position. They do appreciate a little attention. They don't object, for instance, to a tar oil wash in winter, an application of humus and potash in spring, a spray against aphids, mildew, and caterpillars, some pruning back of side shoots in summer, and more rigorous pruning in late autumn, cutting out weak growth, old wood, and crossed branches, besides shortening the lateral shoots.

With June upon us, we are about to thin out the berries for the first gooseberry pie of the season. Later will come pickings for wine. We shall be on the alert for caterpillars, and if we find them, remove them bodily or douse them with derris. If mildew should attack shoots, leaves, or fruit, these will be removed and burnt. A similar fate will befall any aphid-affected shoot tip with curled-in leaves.

Varieties which have been in favour in recent years include Leveller, Whinham's Industry, Whitesmith, Keepsake, and Careless — with Careless apparently in danger of being supplanted by commerical growers who favour a new variety, Invicta, which grows rapidly, is a heavy cropper, resists mildew, and can be on the market slightly earlier than the splendid Careless. Invicta, from East Malling, has among its forbears Whinham's Industry, Keepsake, and Resistenta.

Cheering Wine and Pan Pipes

There is a self-set elderberry sapling at the bottom of my garden — an uninvited guest. Whether to adopt it as a free and future fruit bush or to remove it as a weed is the question of the moment.

Had it been one of its popular relatives, a *viburnum,* for example, promising eventual ornamental flat flower clusters it would have been welcome; but being the common elder, the homely *Sambucus nigra,* it must, I fear, be deemed "below stairs." If it had sprung up on my allotment, there would be no problem because elder and blackberries thrive there without hinder in the boundary hedge.

Some people find the odour of elder wood offputting; and in past times the berries, though eaten by birds, were considered unsuitable for hens and fatal to turkeys and peacocks.

The folk history is fraught with superstition. Gypsies have been known to avoid burning it, hedgecutters to refuse to trim it, not wishing to invite ill luck. Knotted twigs of it have been carried in pockets to prevent rheumatism and crosses of elderwood hung in cow sheds to keep the animals safe. For a plethora of such practices, you need only scan the appropriate pages of Mrs M Grieve's *Modern Herbal.*

Nevertheless, the common elder is a worthy bush. In less finicky times it was much valued for its wood, pith, buds, leaves, flowers, and berries: the wood for skewers, pegs and delicate instruments; the hollow stems to blow up fires, make Pan pipes, popguns and whistles; the smell of the leaves to drive away flies, mice, and moles and — when boiled in a brew — aphids; the flowers for wine, a soothing tea, and also for elderflower water to clear the complexion and soften the skin; the berries for wine, jam, and jelly, and for healthgiving elderberry rub or syrup.

Back in my winemaking days, my wife and I used to make an annual autumn trip to a remote elder of tree-like size growing in swampy ground and producing berries like small grapes. Much nearer home, we also gathered very tiny berries from an almost impenetrable spinney on a chalk hill, and these made much the nicer wine which — years on — I can take out of storage and enjoy.

Here and elsewhere the common elder used to be considered the medicine chest of country dwellers. One doting physician called Boerhaave was said never to pass one without respectfully raising his hat.

As a boy, ill in a Yorkshire farmhouse bedroom facing east, in winter, I can well remember that my mother's elderberry syrup together with a hot water bottle were my close and comforting companions.

Mrs M Grieve gives a recipe for this — wonder syrup or rob (a rob, I learn, is a vegetable or berry juice thickened by heat). You simmer 5lb of fresh ripe berries with 1lb of sugar till the juice is reduced to the thickness of honey; bottle and store for the winter. One, or two tablespoonsful in a tumbler of hot water taken at night promotes perspiration and helps to cure your cold, cough; or flu.

And so... I must decide about my intruding elder sapling. It seems heartless and uneconomic to treat it as a weed. I think I shall transplant it carefully to my allotment, perhaps after a heavy thunder storm, at night, by moonlight, breathing incantations the while and raising my hat in respect.

There it will grow (I hope) unspurned, to rival a healthy and productive specimen on another plot which shades the garden shed and graces the compost heap. Thus, in my dotage, I can fashion popguns and whistles for my great-grandchildren, and sit by the cooker patiently making elderberry ketchup to stimulate my failing taste buds. And since all parts of the elder can be used to make vegetable dyes, I could — if I wished — follow the fashion of the Ancient Romans and dye my grey hair black.

The Plot Thickets

If rhubarb heralds the soft fruit season, the blackberry (Brambleberry, Brummel, or Bumble Kite) brings it to a glorious close; and both are allotment naturals. Even if you don't buy one of the recommended blackberry varieties for your plot, a Bedford Giant or Ashton Cross, you are bound to find a few wild seedlings springing rapidly up and volunteering their services.

When I first took on my rural plot, there was an almost impenetrable bramble thicket at the far end where an aristocratic hare had its home. Even now, I sometimes find myself surprising a reclining hare or leveret along a bean row — probably a descendant of the the line visiting the old ancestral estate.

I tamed that thicket, much bruised, torn, and scratched, and discovered within it two blackberry rows, six feet apart, tied up on stretched wire between posts. And when the fruiting season. arrived, and the scratches were healed, I was overjoyed to be gathering large juicy Bedford and Himalayan Giants.

Alas, those vigorous providers are no longer on the plot. You learn by your mistakes in gardening as elsewhere, especially when you too eagerly throw out the old to introduce the new. My mistake was to remove those noble veterans, and replace them with new thornless varieties, the fruit of which, though plentiful, I find to be late in opening, and reluctant to leave the parent plant, so that you end up with squashed berries and stained fingers.

The idea of reverting to the older varieties, thorns and all, suddenly occurred to me a few weeks ago when our neighbouring plot on the northern side became overgrown with nettles, bindweed, and brambles, threatening invasion — one of the hazards of allotmenteering. Long briars were bending in graceful curves out of the jungle and over the border to take an adventurous look at our more open space. With great cunning, therefore, I decided to tip-layer these in our own soil, sinking the briar tips a few inches into the ground. Thus, I argued, by late autumn I should have new blackberry plants of known quality.

Unfortunately, I hadn't let Nelson, my plot associate, know what I was about, and the next time I met him on the plot, he was perspiring freely, and clearing our border country with commendable octogenarian energy, briars and all.

Autumn is a good planting time for black and hybrid berries, unless it is too wet, in which case spring would be better. A soft fruit conference at Stockbridge House Experimental Horticultural Station revealed useful berry information, with comparative facts and figures, aimed chiefly at commercial growers in the north, but not overlooking the amateur small gardener who searches for good ideas and practical advice.

The Bedford Giant, for instance (bred by Laxtons of Bedford half a century ago with a raspberry somewhere among its forbears), has given a consistently higher yield than any other berry, black or hybrid, over the past six years at Stockbridge House. It ripens early, has large round fruits, freezes well, and seems not to be bothered much by pests or diseases. Ashton Cross is also high yielding, with a wild blackberry flavour. Oregon Thornless is less heavy cropping but is friendlier to deal with. Himalayan Giant, on the other hand, is vigorous and, as I well remember, inclined to fight back with vicious swipes when you attempt to prune it and tie up the young briars.

The hybrid berries have interesting possibilities for the small gardener. One of our plot holders has a very successful Tayberry with a large purple-red fruit. The Tummelberry is a cross between a Tayberry and one of its seedlings with rounder and redder fruits. It is said to be hardier than Tayberry and may yield better after a hard winter. The Sunberry has glossy black fruits of good flavour. Thornless Boysonberry (a Californian hybrid of

135

unknown parentage) is not fully hardy in our north where it is inclined to be low in yield, but is said to be one of the finest flavoured of cane fruits for any amateur who feels inclined to try it. But it is the Marionberry (also from the US) which, though not fully hardy in severe winters, is likely, when trained on a trellis, to please the small gardener for its large white flowers in June and its sweetly flavoured fruits in July-August.

Expert advice in planting, given at the conference, is to choose your site carefully (boundary fences, rustic arch ways, pergolas, sheds, and old tree stumps are all possibilities for the more attractive berries) prepare the ground thoroughly, dig deeply, remove perennial weeds, incorporate well rotted manure, put a little moisture-retaining peat at the bottom of the planting holes, remove with sharp secateurs any broken and diseased roots, plant fairly deeply, firm and level off, cut the canes down to nine inches and — if sufficiently strong willed — don't let them fruit in the first season. After harvest, advice is to remove the old canes close to the base, tie up the new ones with soft jute string, cut out thin and broken canes, and hoe out suckers. Hoeing round the plants should be shallow.

The fact that blackberries and hybrid berries are largely free from disease and pest attacks is something to be acknowledged with quiet but fervent thankfulness.

Strawberry Fields

Strawberries are infinitely desirable and generally rewarding on an allotment if you are able to give them the care and attention they demand and deserve; that is to say, if you can plant good stock while the ground is still warm, observe the rules, avoid full shade and drought, thwart the pests, escape the diseases, and keep off the wild rabbits.

Leslie, a plot neighbour, observes the cultivation rules and is successful. He met me on my return to the plots in early July with a gift of large juicy berries cupped in a rhubarb leaf.

Leslie's plants are in their second year. In their first, he courageously removed all the flower trusses with scissors, to be rewarded this year with an excellent crop. He used to grow Royal Sovereign, that veteran variety bred by Thomas Laxton (of Laxton apples) in 1892 — the only recommended variety to survive the second world war.

In the first world war — a time of frugal eating — I well remember roaming woodlands in North Oxfordshire in search of those tiny but tasty wild strawberries. The early New England colonists, in their distress, had done likewise, taught by the American Indians to mix them with maize flour and so make wild strawberry bread.

The large garden strawberries were, it seems, unknown to the ancients and subsequent centuries. Stafford Whiteaker, in his excellent and delightfully illustrated book, *The Compleat Strawberry*, tells of the modern strawberry's development in the last two centuries or so; how a Frenchman in South America dug up some larger fruiting plants he found at the foot of the Andes near Quito *(Fragaria chiloensis)* to take home to France; how he shared his ration of drinking water with these plants on his six month voyage; and how five of his plants survived to arrive at Marseilles in August 1712, there to found a stock of Chilean strawberries. Two plants went to royal gardens in Paris, and from their progeny Philip Miller, "the Prince of Gardeners", had received plants at our Chelsea Physic Garden by 1726.

It was an enlightened young French man, Antoine Duchesne, who first experimented with the hybridisation of strawberries, followed eventually by others like Michael Keens, a market gardener of Isleworth whose Keens's Seedling — large of berry and finely flavoured became the parent of our modern strawberry.

Ken Muir and Chris Bower are two strawberry specialists of today. Ken Muir's stand at the Chelsea Flower Show has always repaid a visit with berries hanging from baskets and growing in tubs, and specimens of Alpines and summerlong fruiting Perpetuals. His recently revised booklet, *Growing Strawberries For Pleasure*, has cultivation advice and 30 recommended varieties with notes about each.

Just as Royal Sovereign once reigned supreme and has declined, so Cambridge Favourite now gives way to newer varieties. Mr Muir says that one of these, Elsanta, has become the market leader in Europe within the short space of three years because of its longer shelf life, firmness, good shape, and flavour. Elsanta is now arriving from the Netherlands out of season and in large quantities, either being forced for the early market or deliberately held back in cold storage to be planted in the field for cropping during August and September.

My plot neighbour, however, is likely to stay loyally and patriotically with Cambridge Favourite, though he is tempted to try a new variety alongside and compare results — say Grandee or Pantagruella from West Germany, or Bounty from Canada, or Hapil from Belgium, or Elsanta from the Netherlands — but not on land following potatoes. Or he might try Fraises des Bois, a non runnering Alpine, or Rapella, which is also a Perpetual with larger berries that begin ripening earlier. And now is a good time to decide.

Myself, I have given up growing strawberries as being too difficult for me to keep weedfree, but I can still admire the growers of this delightfully refreshing berry that for some reason best known to itself carries its seeds on the outside of the fruit.

Coming Up Rosy

It is rhubarb that heralds the new allotment year. Rosy-cheeked, staunch, and upstanding, it burgeons forth in rain or shine, frost or fog, hail or snow.

How it can show such colour and glowing health when all around is vegetatively cold and miserable is a mystery to me. Perhaps its ancestor, the *Rheum rhaponticum* of Siberia, has endowed it with fortitude.

I contend that the Timperley Early variety on my plot is already providing a substitute for those more tardy and weather conscious soft fruits which will keep me queueing up till June and July.

Introduced into this country in 1573, it is held in high esteem by the average Briton. Other nationalities will learn to like it. The Victorian kitchen garden always had its rhubarb corner. Varieties bearing the names Victoria and Prince Albert are still with us: sturdy, enduring, respected. Prince Albert blooms profusely but the flower heads should be removed without delay.

Effortlessly forced under bins, boxes, barrels, buckets, or under polythene, rhubarb on the allotment quickly becomes pullable; especially if you remembered to give it a dressing of farmyard manure in late autumn and intend to give it a nitrogen fertiliser in the spring. I already enjoy juvenile sticks from my own plot, stewed and eaten with custard, or with chopped dates and ginger.

Pulling while young seems not to damage the crown or reduce the yield.

South Yorkshire is the heartland of rhubarb country. Stockbridge House Experimental Horticultural Station, at Cawood, specialises in the research and development of the crop, while the Northern Horticultural Society's Harlow Car Gardens hold the National Rhubarb Collection from whose genetic base breeding material can be selected.

At Stockbridge House they work to produce varieties with low acid and high sugar content which retain their red stick colour and shape after bottling; their crowns produce sticks with good flavour which remain firm and straight after forcing.

Traditional propagation means splitting two-year-old crowns into sets in the autumn, but they also experiment with rapid propagation methods in pots. Micropropagation of rhubarb, however, is said to have only limited success so far.

Cawood Delight, of unknown parentage, is bred at Stockbridge House and finds a happy home on an allotment. It is at its best from the middle of May until early July. The sticks are rather short and of a deep maroon colour which is not lost in cooking. It freezes well.

Stockbridge Arrow which has small arrowshaped leaves and very straight stems, is good for forcing by the commercial growers.

Stockbridge Harbinger, a seedling from Timperley Early, is a little later than its forebear but earlier than Prince Albert and claimed to be superior to both.

Other varieties have been tried at Stockbridge House, including Cawood Oak, Cawood Castle and Cawood Ensign, as well as the more nationally known names.

Steins Champagne is considered to be a variety second to none as a culinary rhubarb because of its delicate pinkness, and supurb flavour. It was grown on a market garden near York for many years and has since been virus-tested.

Cardinal Wolsey is a promising early variety. (Little Cawood is large with history. Cardinal Wolsey was arrested there in the Archbishop's Palace in 1530: "Farewell, a long farewell to all my greatness...")

It's a Good Old Bean

You can sow broad beans of one kind or another throughout most of the year. Last year on the allotment we did very well from April-sown Giant Windsors, which were easy, and considerably less well from some overwintered Aquadulce Claudia, which were difficult, demanding protection from wind and weather, and revealing too many gaps in the row. Sheltered gardens are understandably another story, but open allotments have their private problems.

Some plot neighbours sow in January–February, to beat the blackfly, but later-sown beans can also escape it if you remember to top the plants as soon as pods begin to set. Dwarf varieties can be sown up to July. Regrettably the Sutton Dwarf, on which I have depended in past seasons, is not this year available, but Dobies list their award-winning Midget and Marshall's of Wisbech their semi-dwarf Staygreen, which they claim to have "near-sugar-pea" flavour. Of course, all broad beans if gathered young enough can, like the sugar pea, be cooked and eaten pod and all.

The broad bean is my favourite bean. It is of sterling character and attractive appearance. An affection for it develops in early schooldays when those jam-jars lined with moist blotting paper on classroom window-ledges first reveal the marvels of germination and growth. Nothing can bring more charm to a vegetable garden in spring than trim rows of sturdy infant beans, looking so perkily healthy and so confident that all in the vegetable world is wonderful.

They grow well on any fertile soil. They are reliable. They are protein-laden. Harvested and dried, they and their relatives the field beans have helped man and beast to survive hard winters across many centuries. And they owe nothing to the New World. I have yet to meet a US citizen who can identify them, or who is familiar with the name. "You must mean Lima beans," they sometimes say, inaccurately.

Broad beans are therefore genuine Old World beans, going back, archaeologists say, to Ancient Egypt and the Bronze Age. In the beginning they must have been hard and unattractive; our plant breeders are to be thanked for the improved varieties of today.

There are two sorts, Longpods (which include the Sutton Dwarf) and Windsors, both of which have white-seeded and green-seeded varieties. Longpods are recommended for overwintering and Windsors are good for the spring. In flavour, the whites and greens are alike, but the greens are said to be increasingly popular because they freeze better, and because people want colour in their vegetables these days.

The various combinations are a little confusing but a good catalogue helps. I sometimes feel the need for an alert child, catalogue in hand, to test me on, say, the differences between Suttons' Masterpiece Green Longpod and their Unrivalled Green Windsor; or between Dobies' Imperial White Windsor and their Promotion Early Longpod.

Last year I grew treble rows in the hope that closer ranks would make for better defence against strong winds, but the hope proved vain; all varieties except the dwarfs do need the support of enclosing string fastened to stakes. Some think it advisable to saw the seeds individually with a blunt-ended dibber to a depth of three inches, so as to thwart the mice who find drills easy guide-lines for the depredations.

A plot neighbour sprinkles loose earth over the young beans as they come through, claiming that this light soil falls in the faces of predators and puts them off. Others prefer to start off their beans in cold frames for planting out later.

John Loudon, that gardening sage of Victorian times, recommended in those pre-freezer days a method of retardation to get later crops: namely, to cut the bean plants back, a few inches from the ground, at the stage when they are about to blossom, thus causing new stems to appear and so to bring a delayed crop, or even a very early crop the following year. I intend to test this out on the allotment. Normally, of course, side-shoots are nipped out, not encouraged.

The Dutch, I gather, sow summer savoury among their beans, in the first place to drive away blackfly, and afterwards to use the herb for flavouring the cooked beans. Also I read — but cannot confirm — that beans benefit from the neighbourliness of carrots and beet, but abhor the close company of onions, garlic and shallots.

Field beans are said to be happier when befriended by oats. For myself, I am never happier than when enjoying fresh garden broad beans with white sauce, or fried with bacon; and with survival in mind, I'm sure I shall be able to take to dried beans, well soaked and turned into soup, or ground into protein-rich bean meal for baking.

Allotment Wines

It is a short step for an allotmenteer to become a home winemaker, if only to use up the surplus fruit, vegetables, and weeds that sometimes lie around. Yes, even weeds; for some people make nettle wine, some brew nettle beer, and others prize the winemakine properties of dandelion, coltsfoot, and clover.

Fermented drink has a history going back to Ancient Persia if not to neolithic times: and it is quite mistaken to suppose that wine is always *vin,* and made from grapes. With allotment produce you can make drinkable wine from gooseberries, parsnips and all soft fruits; from spinach, pars!ey, carrots, beetroot, broad beans, celery, and even peapods; from ripe tomatoes, rhubarb, maize, and apples. And with pickings from your plot or from nearby hedgerows you may exploit the winemaking potentials of rose petals, may blossom, white pinks, and elder flowers.

My own addiction started soon after taking up an allotment a few years ago, so that now I am able to drink my own table wines daily without fear of the cellar running dry. Other people who show an interest may sample it, though I never press it on visitors — partly out of modesty but more out of bottle unpredictability. Only once, however, have I pulled a wry face and emptied a bottle down the drain. Gooseberry I rate as best, with parsnip a close second. Apple and blackberry also please my palate.

At the risk of being knocked down by more proficient amateurs, I would say that wine-making is not difficult if you use gallon fermenting jars fitted with airlocks in the corks, if you put them in the airing cupboard in winter, and if you seek recipes and advice from the public library shelves under 641.87 of the Dewey system (next to the cookbooks). From there on you can begin to learn from experience and introduce a little originality.

My own efforts make necessary some intrusions into the kitchen, where I am not always popular; I usually leap into wine making action when my wife goes out of the house, and hope to have cleaned up the stains and expelled the yeasty smells before her return. Only once have the walls and ceiling been spattered by an expensive "must." Happy is the person who has their own winery.

Published recipes seem usually to suggest generous quantities of ingredients which produce sweet, dessert type wines. By reducing these quanties by almost a half, I find I can make thinner and drier table wines — about two pounds of sugar to the gallon, for instance, and less fruit than is usually suggested. And since yeast needs a little help to do its job (of reacting on the sugar to produce alcohol and give off carbon dioxide), I always add the recommended boosters. I aim at high standards of cleanliness, using campden tablets and a pinch of citric acid in solution as a sterilising agent.

Herewith my wine making prospectus. In January I shall dig up some frosted parsnips from my plot (frosted parsnips are best), scrub, slice, steep, strain and put them in the fermenting jar with the yeast, to be racked after three weeks and again a month or so later, and then left in the dark for a further few weeks before bottling.

In February I shall limber up for the sap-tapping season, to catch a birch or sycamore in March when the vital juice is rising but while the leaf buds are still asleep, unaware and unharmed by this minor molestation. (Queen Victoria, I understand, made her sap wine from silver birches on the Balmoral estate.)

In April I shall be watching out for the flowers of elder and dandelion, followed by the catching of the rhubarb at its best in May. Green gooseberries will follow in June and July, with the soft fruits and the option of experimenting with peapod and parsley. In August and September my allotment blackberries are at their best, and in October my sweetcorn should be fermentable.

146

In November I may be tempted to bring out stored carrots and beetroot for the brew and in December, after a wine year hopefully well spent. I plan to sit at the fireside, drinking tea and saving the surplus from the pot; because tea wine, they say, if properly made, can compete with sherry. By which time, seeking new worlds to conquer, I shall probably be planning to keep bees, gather honey, and make mv own fermentations of mead, pyment. hypocras, melomel and cyser.

In Praise of the Noble Spud

At this time of year, as the mornings brighten and the days lengthen, it is tempting to rise early and reach my rural allotment to surprise the birds and beasts at their tricks. They regard my plot as their own territorial preserve during these unwanted hours. On my arrival, however, the wildlife discreetly departs with the exception of the robin and the blackbird who expect me to prepare their breakfast by turning over a few spits.

I can then inspect the plot to see if my newly planted-out sugar peas have been pecked at, the spring cabbages grazed, the onion sets uprooted, the carefully prepared brassica seedbed scratched over, or the more tender herbs demolished. All these I have protected — not as diligently, alas as some of my neighbours — with netting, wire, and plastic, sometimes supported by plastic cups on canes, with prickly twigs and thorny branches. We lack the boy scarers of bygone days. But we do have a resident sparrow hawk.

To herald the new season I have treated myself to a handsome garden line. Hitherto, a length of string tied to two sticks has served myself and Nelson well enough. As a diehard allotmenteer I am aware of but never use metric measure on the plot. My foot is a foot, three make a yard, 5 yards make a rod, pole or perch, and ten square rods make a standard allotment — roughly 30 yards by ten, or 302½ square yards to be exact. I think. What that is in square metres I shall never hope to know. Our allotments were mapped out in ten rod plots. No doubt most other allotments were as well and there seems no pressing need to change. We on the plots respect the past and time-tested methods.

Following my experimental no-dig year — which, all told, was for me a disaster — I have now, thanks to favourable weather, returned to normal. By dint of small stints, with long rest in between, I have enjoyed the digging and am delighted to find that I can rake the soil to a fine tilth once more for seed sowing. And in the intervals of resting outside the hut, I can breathe delicious fresh air, enjoy the intermittent sunshine, compile a lengthy mental list of jobs to be done, and be thankful for my lot.

Last year I planted my potatoes by trowelling holes in the hard ground. They cropped quite well. In fact, potato planting can help to break up new ground. This year, however, I am glad to revert to our accustomed method while planting my Arran Pilots and Pentland Javelins. (Earlies are not so long in the ground as maincrops and are therefore less vulnerable to slugs).

I begin with a 6in trench for the first row, using my new garden line, apply farmyard manure or other fertiliser, cover with a little soil, plant the earlies a foot apart in rows 2ft apart, working backwards and turning the soil as I go.

Believing that gardeners should never hurry, I pause frequently to straighten my back and ponder the enormous debt we owe to this important vegetable and how we take it for granted or, even worse, refer to it as a spud. We should know more about the *Solanum tuberosum,* about its chequered history and importance to humanity.

Not all the story is rosy, of course. The *Solanum tuberosum* has had its ups and downs. We can hardly condone, for instance, the action of the Incas — the original possessors of the potato — for using human blood as a sacrificial fertiliser. Nor can we, or must we, ever forget those terrible years of 1845 and 1846 when blight struck the Irish crop, when so many people starved and survivors emigrated to America.

Less upsetting but none the less surprising were first reactions to this strange vegetable when it arrived in Europe. The Burgundians blamed it for cancer, the Prussians for tuberculosis, while the Russians abhorred it as food from the devil. Our own Brave Queen Bess,

149

however, not only risked eating potatoes but actually enjoyed them and soon the aristocracy were poaching them in wine and decorating them with truffles. Marie Antoinette wore potato flowers in her hair, Louis XVI as a buttonhole, while the French Revolutionaries turned the Palace Gardens into a potato field.

Then there is the story of Fluke, a Victorian variety, one of twelve potato plants grown by a Lancashire weaver from a seedpod or "potato plum" nicked from a potato field in 1841. In a few years this white skinned, pink eyed Fluke was being commonly grown and Fluke's natural seedling Victoria is a forbear of some of today's varieties.

Statistics — always surprising — show that on average we eat 242lb of potatoes per head each year; that the price is about four times what it was in 1860; that in a sample of 2,244 people, 74 per cent agreed that you need potatoes to make a proper meal; and that the vitamin and mineral content is commendable.

Long live the noble spud!

Cabbages in Depth

The Romans appear to have liked cabbages. The poet Horace included them in his kitchen garden. Cato is said to have adored them. And the Emperor Diocletian, worn out with cares of state, retired into the country to cultivate them.

It is now almost a year since I followed this noble Roman example and took an allotment in the country, resolved on growing a steady supply of greens, particularly for the winter months. The auspices were good. The patch of wilderness allotted to me last February happened to be near a well-kept plot abounding in good-looking winter greens. So I bought my brassica seeds, restive for sowing time. But the chill winds of March drove me indoors, giving me time, so to speak, to research cabbages.

I began with the *Oxford Dictionary,* seeking the precise definition: Cabbage — a well-known culinary vegetable: a plane-leaved cultivated variety of Brassica oleracea, the unexpanded leaves of which form a compact globular heart or head.

Next, I looked for origins. The wild cabbage, seemingly, is native to these sea-girt islands, being neither brought in by the Romans nor accompanied by the Conqueror. The cultivated cabbage was to be found on all good medieval allotments.

By the early 1700s several varieties were being grown, including the Russian Cabbage, the Sugar-loaf Cabbage, the Flat-sided Cabbage, the Turnip-rooted Cabbage, the Battersea, and the Boor Cole. A century later, the Battersea Cabbage was still going strong, while the Early Imperial Brompton was vuying with the Early Russian, the Early Sugar-loaf, and the Early Emperor.

Of course not all cabbages by name are cabbages by nature. To the question, "When is a cabbage not a cabbage?" one must answer, "When it is an Arkansas

Cabbage, or a Bastard Cabbage, or a Chinese Cabbage, or a Dog Cabbage, or a Skunk Cabbage (which smells of garlic), or St Patrick's Cabbage (London Pride), or Sea-otter Cabbage, which is a very interesting seaweed of the North-west Pacific coast. Nor is the Cabbage Tree true cabbage. It is a palm; though its terminal bud is eaten as a cabbage in some parts of the world.

But to return to my own cabbage-garth where (the winds being warmer) I sowed my selected brassica seeds — cabbage, cauliflowers, broccoli, and brussels sprouts — in a seed-bed, marking the rows with wooden labels clearly names in biro ink. It was here that my real troubles began. In the first place, the labels, after a heavy shower, were washed clean.

The young plants fell foul of most of the ailments that cabbage flesh is heir to, so that I bitterly regretted not having researched rather the cabbage caterpillar, cabbage root fly, cabbage white fly, and flea beetle. All these scourges made me turn gratefully to calomel dust and Derris. But the brassicas bravely withstood all hazards, including, more recently, strong winds from the North which bent them badly towards the South.

"Shallow planting!" I said to myself censoriously, making a note to plant more deeply next time, and to earth up the stalks for greater support.

However, in spite of all setbacks, my wilderness of last February has become a blessing of winter greens. It is nice to have them to turn to. They serve us well. After a good meal of winter greens I find I can the more readily return to my researches. Much remains for me to do in the cabbage field. I badly want, for instance, to investigate Smith O'Brien's cabbage-garden rebellion. And then there is cabbage-in-the-vernacular to be explored. What, for example, is one to make of the dialect expression, "He's as green as a yalla cabbish"? I feel I ought to know.

Corn on the Compost

My wife and I grow sweet corn on our allotment, chiefly because we cherish memories of corn-on-the-cob suppers we once ate by candlelight with friends in New England. There the corn is at its best in August, boiled with salt, spread lavishly with butter, held horizontally before the mouth with special finger-prongs and nibbled at rodent-like.

Last year we under-achieved, as the educationalists say about those whom the gods love but do not specially favour. Our seed corn, planted in May, took an interminable time to sprout, and did so only when the weather got warmer. At first the young plants resembled couch grass; then, during June and July, they began to develop their own character and personality, producing long wavy leaves like pennants flying on the breeze; but we had to admit we had seen better specimens for the time of year. In Italy, for instance, in that northern province of Friuli, where the rain falls every afternoon at half-past three, followed by a fiery sun showering his golden beams on the teeming earth, the corn grows twelve feet high. But on our allotment it was not an inch above four.

It was towards the end of August that Connie came to view the allotment. Connie is an American friend who lives in England and was recently in Nepal. When she arrived at the plot we deliberately paused at the "grand gateway" formed by our two clumps of corn. But, alas, she overlooked it — literally. We had to draw her attention to it. And when she looked down and saw it, she was obviously taken aback. "I guess it's not as high as an elephant's eye," she said, enigmatically, after a pause; and then, "Is it a dwarf variety?"

I said it was a variety known as "Golden Early." The name seemed to surprise her: "Did you say early?"

Sheepishly, I asked her how tall the maize corn grew in Nepal. "Fifteen feet," she said without flinching.

However, we soldiered on, never losing patience or giving up hope: and by September our corn was really trying hard. Ears were detected growing from the main stems. Then silky threads emerged from these ears.

This was the pistolate inflorescence. Next, the flowers on top of the stalks opened out in display (the staminate inflorescence) and the result was corn cobs which, though diminutive by American standards, we harvested, cooked, and nibbled in the New England manner.

This year we tried new methods, aiming at accelerated growth. Early in May we put the seed corn in Jiffy-pots, in compost, in the airing cupboard; and during the remarkably brief sprouting period of two or three days we remembered the Pilgrim Fathers who owed their survival to an Indian-corn granary hidden beneath the sand dunes of Cape Cod.

The Indians told them the corn should be sown when the young leaves of the oak were as big as the ears of a mouse; and that, we detected, was in mid-May. For best results, said the Indians, you should compost in the soil round the roots a few small fish, such as they found washed up on the beaches. (Ale-wives, the Americans call these fish.) And, finally, you should scoop out a soil bowl at the base of each stem to collect rain.

With these points noted, we went to work. In the absence of ale-wives we at first thought of sardines, or pilchards, perhaps; but we settled for some well-rotted compost mixed with a general fertiliser, at the same time making a mental note to give applications of fish manure later on. For each plant I first removed rather more than a spade's depth of soil, forked loose the subsoil, poured a bucket of water into the hole, filled it with compost and planted the corn in its Jiffy-pot, firmed well down till it was sitting comfortably in the middle of its rain-receiving bowl.

The plants made a row along the front of the plot, alternating rather effectively with small bushes of potentilla. They made a good start, looked a good colour in June, sturdy in July, and aesthetically attractive thereafter, making with their yellow-blooming neighbours a pleasant border. And in due course we gathered corn cobs of improved 1970 size and quality, to boil with salt, spread lavishly with butter, hold horizontally before the mouth with special finger-prongs, and nibble at, rodent-like, by candlelight. As we did so, we thought of the Indians to whom the corn meant so much, and of the Pilgrim Fathers to whom it meant even more.

Artichoke Pie

When I was a boy, living in the country, there were Jerusalem artichokes growing in the garden, I remember. They were wild and free, rampaging through a shrubbery and heading for the orchard. I used to imagine they had been brought to England by returning Crusaders; but now, half a century later (with a country allotment at my feet and a fancy to grow artichokes in my head), I have learned differently.

The Jerusalem artichoke, strictly speaking, is not an artichoke. It must not be confused with the true artichoke, variously styled as the Globe, Common, Green, Italian, French, or Paris artichoke. It is not even Mediterranean in origin; it is American. It is a species of sunflower or rasole, whereas the true artichoke is related to the thistle.

The *Encyclopaedia Britannica,* with a heartless display of character assassination, states that, above ground, the Jerusalem artichoke is a coarse, usually much-branched, frost-tender annual, six to ten feet tall, with underground tubers which have no food value for people or beasts. None the less, the *Helianthus tuberosus* has an interesting, if somewhat chequered history.

In or about 1600, it seems, questing white people saw them growing in the gardens and allotments of North American Indians and brought them to our shores. The Farnese Gardens in Rome grew them under the name of *Girasole articiocco* because the tubers had an artichoke flavour. "And from this *girasole* we have made Jerusalem; and from Jerusalem artichokes we make "Palestine soup," as readers of "Gryll Grange" will probably not remember. And not only soup: artichoke pies were made with marrows, dates, ginger, raisins, and sherry sack.

I have only once in my life tasted Jerusalem artichokes, and that was half a century ago. The memory of the taste across that span of time remains vivid and objectionable.

But so did the taste of parsnips until last year, when I grew my own on the allotment and became very partial to them. I hope, therefore, for a similar comeback with the Jerusalems this year.

But when I asked for Jerusalem artichoke sets at the village gardening shop, the young woman seemed to suspect some kind of practical joke — like being asked for a pound of rubber nails. Nor did I fare better when I rang up a near-by nurseryman. "No demand" was his firm and final response. I tried next — several times — a specialist seedsman. He was at first confident of getting a consignment, though from the outset he didn't disguise his fears that severe frost might have got them first. In the event, it had. I inquired at the horticultural establishments of several market towns, but without hope. It was on my mind to write to a North American Indian.

However, my wife had a telephone conversation with a kind and resourceful sister in Lincolnshire. Lincolnshire is a county of character: it has not wantonly severed its roots in a rural and honourable past, nor has it cast all its Jerusalem artichokes to perdition. They are grown, nowadays, as a cover for pheasants. The pheasants nest in them, I understand, and even nibble at them, which shows what connoisseurs they are.

And so a carefully packed parcel of Jerusalem artichoke tubers arrived by first class mail, and I hastened with them to the allotment. And there — following the advice of one John Sanders in his *Kitchen Garden Directory* of 1827 — I found some rich and mellow ground in which to plant them, four inches deep and 18 inches apart. Following the same advice, when they appear I shall clear away the weeds, draw up the soil to the bottom of the stems, watch the tops grow six to ten feet tall, gather the crop in October or November and then, with all appropriate ritual, bake that seventeeth-century artichoke pie. I can hardly wait.

Pepper Proud

This has been in interesting year for allotment exotica. My wife and I have played host to an assortment of aubergines or egg-plants, peppers (capsicum and chili), custard marrows, and ornamental gourds. A cantaloupe melon called "Sweetheart" turned out to be too shy to face an allotment environment, but the gourds pulled through to become a lusty proliferating lot, much given to aggrandisement. They festooned themselves over the hawthorn hedge at the end of the plot and adorned the adjacent Jerusalem artichokes. The peppers, on the other hand, were discreet, unassuming, co-operative, and always interesting. The peppers were our favourites.

Peppers, unlike rhubarb or radishes, do not immediately strike you as a likely allotment crop. Nevertheless, there is good reason to grow them, especially if the horticultural compendium I was looking at the other day is not wildly out of date or off the mark. The frequent adulteration of red pepper with red lead and other poisonous substances, it averred "renders the cultivation of the capsicum in gardens for a home supply very desirable." Which makes me thankful that we have capsicum and to spare.

While doing my homework on them I learned that peppers are many and various, even if you exclude the *Piper nigrum* from which the black and white peppers of commerce are produced. There are Bell and Bull-nosed peppers, for instance; and Bird pepper.

Then — to rival the butterflies — there is the Long Yellow Capsicum, the Purple Capsicum, the American Bonnet, and the Spanish Mammoth. Then, of course, there are the hotter chili or Guinea or Cayenne peppers — sometimes also called red peppers or pod peppers.

It was last winter that I put all pepper research on one side, opened a seed catalogue and plumped, without more

158

ado, for one packet of "Capsicum (Sweet Peppers, Mixed)" and one packet of "Chili (Cayenne Pepper)." These packets arrived in wintry February; and without delay I sowed them in trays of seed compost.

A month or so later, I was busy pricking out perky 2in-high plants into 3in-diameter pots, from which, by early summer, they had graduated to larger pots and were ready to go out into the world to seek their fortunes.

I planted some in open ground, left some in their pots, and gave all the benefit of allotment glass and plenty of water. They grew into attractive plants, some sturdy of stem, others more graceful, rather bushy, and with white five-pointed starlets for flowers. In August and September they began to fruit, some with large, variously-shaped, fleshy green peppers which would ripen to red or yellow.

It was then that there came to pass two happenings of great joy. One was the unusually warm Indian summer of early October, which brought a belated ripening blush to our heavy clusters of green tomatoes. The other, quite plot-shaking in impact, was the news that the local horticultural society had recommended our allotment for acclaim as the "Best Improved Garden of the Village." We received the news with befitting calm and sobriety, against the certain knowledge that soon a frost would come, a killing frost, to nip our exotics and bring low all high-blown pride and vaunting ambition.

And so it befell. Luckily the custard marrows and ornamental gourds had outlived their natural life-span, leaving behind them a colourful collection of mocking progeny to bedeck and bedazzle the kitchen.

The peppers, however, were still in their prime and disinclined to die. With all speed, therefore, we brought them in out of the cold, back to the crowded window-sill scenes of their childhood, where they now offer on all sides a choice of green or red peppers for the pot. The problem of window-sill overcrowding, at first a worry, is now happily resolved: we shall give the pepper plants as Christmas presents — wherever possible, in advance.

Harvest of Love Apples

It has been a delight this warm summer and tranquil early autumn to watch the tomatoes ripening in the open. My few bush and cherry toms have seemed to blush almost as you look at them. And the Autumn Bliss rasps which began ripening in spring have continued, true to their name, into October.

When a flower, fruit or vegetable distinguishes itself in some way on my plot, I like to learn more about its origins and development.

Take tomatoes, the Lycopersicum (wolf peach — a misnomer) esculentum (edible) of the Solanaceae (potato family). It seems that all our varieties — large or small, thick or thin-skinned, cheery, pear, plum, or peach-shaped, flat and crinkled or globular and smooth, red or yellow, greenhouse or outdoor — all derive from the wild tomato berry growing on the lower western slopes of the Andes in South America and first domesticated in Mexico.

When it reached Europe, six years after Columbus discovered America, it was known as the Peruvian, Golden, or Love Apple and was thereupon grown and eaten by the carefree Italians, although suspected it was poisonous. Eventually it spread to France, Germany and England, but was still regarded with suspicion by the colonists of North America. Gerard, the Elizabethan English herbalist, catalogued and grew it in his own Holborn garden as a decorative and medicinal herb. It was a couple of centuries before this botanical berry was grown in the States, the US Supreme Court adjusting it to vegetable status in 1893.

Over the years, the plant breeders and researchers have produced by hybridisation and selection more and more varieties, mainly with the aim of giving us larger, more uniform, shapely, heavier yielding, and more disease-resisting cultivars. Mr Alan Balch in Ayrshire introduced the popular Ailsa Craig. Then there have been the mutations or "sports" like Becker's Devon Surprise producing cream instead of green coloured unripened fruit, and Jones' Outdoor Prolific with potato-like leaves and flat, pink fruits.

Two decades ago when I took on my allotment and tried to grow a few tomatoes on it, I used Ailsa Craig plants and a few Dutch lights given to me by Pip, the market gardener over the hedge, along with advice on how to handle them. (Use two hands to move them and never lift them by a corner or the glass will break). They have long since gone – shattered by gales or lifted absent-mindedly at a corner – but they were useful while they lasted, four to make good open access frames, two to lean against each other like an inverted V, or singly rested on bricks.

But in this phenomenal year they have not been needed. My six tomato plants - two Sigmabush (Suttons), two Red Alert, and two Gardener's Delight, were germinated in the airing cupboard, put into individual pots within 10 days of germination, planted out in sheltered corners in the first week of June in heavily-manured soil from last year, and then left largely to make their own way. The aim was to compare them for flavour yield, and ripening.

Sigmabush has given by far the heaviest crop and was first to ripen, but was not the winner for flavour. As last year, I have hung the uprooted plants in a dry place for gradual ripening of the few green ones left. Gardener's Delight and Red Alert were flavoursome.

Gardening Which? has reported on 13 tomato varieties. They were given the same greenhouse treatment and then tested by 400 people. They found that the three most popular varieties, Ailsa Craig, Alicante and Moneymaker, did less well than Herald, Sioux and Gemini, while Gardener's Delight was top for taste and Danny the heaviest cropper.

I would guess that all varieties have been tastier this year, thanks to our increased ration of sunshine. Not all crops have liked the heat, however. My marrows and courgettes have, certainly, but the sweet peas were disappointing and quickly over. Desirée potatoes have been good, but not brassicas. Beans have been prolific, as were the soft fruits at midsummer.

Miracle Comfrey

Is comfrey a wonder plant? Mr Lawrence D. Hills of the
Henry Doubleday Research Association makes me believe
that it is; and if so, why am I not growing it on my
allotment as a kitchen vegetable, medicinal herb, and
green manure? I really must send off to the HDRA for six
comfrey offsets at once. Bocking No. 14 is the
recommended variety for gardeners, and planting can be
done in any month of the year except December and
January.

Comfrey, I read, is a quick-growing perennial which
"draws up from the sub-soil the plant foods that are
beyond the reach of anything but a tree." This herculean
prowess on the part of a herb daunts me a little, I confess,
because I have had trouble in times past with fork-bending
rhubarb crowns, un-get-riddable Jerusalem artichokes,
and stubbornly deep-rooted parsnips.

Fortunately, my fears seem to be unfounded. Mr Hills
explains how easily you can get rid of it — should you
become so ill-advised as to wish to do so — by simply
cutting it at the root and applying a little sodium chlorate
weedkiller. If, on the other hand, you wish to have and to
hold comfrey, to cherish it, and to grow it as a vegetable,
medicine or manure (or indeed as chicken, horse or cattle
feed), you plant your new offsets two feet apart each way
in a sunny bed cleared of grass, docks and dandelions.
Thereafter your comfrey requires nothing more than clean
cultivation, nitrogenous food and regular cutting during
the growing season. The young leaves may be eaten in
early spring as spinach, and the young shoots as
asparagus.

Medicinally and dietetically, says Mr Hills, comfrey's
value lies in the cell proliferant allantoin, and in the fact
that it contains — mainly in the stem and apparently
uniquely in the plant world — vitamin B12. The fresh

163

leaves and mucilaginous roots were, I believe, used by the ancients on the battlefield to bandage and heal wounds; nowadays they are included in the manufacture of comfrey ointment and comfrey cream. The fresh leaves may be chopped into "tea," ground into "flour," or compressed into tablets to be taken internally. In one form or another, comfrey has been variously claimed to cure rasped throats, coughs, quinsy, chronic intestinal trouble, asthma, bronchitis, hay fever, bed sores, chicken pox, swollen toes, athlete's foot, corns, varrucas and chilblains, and to help in healing all manner of sprains, breaks and bruises thus earning from early times names like bone-set and bruisewort.

As a green manure or "instant compost," wilted comfrey is claimed to have considerably higher rates of nitrogen and phosphorous than farmyard manure, and a much higher content of potash. It is therefore particularly good for potash-greedy plants like gooseberries, potatoes and tomatoes, and a godsend to organic gardeners.

Yes, I shall write off immediately to HDRA, not only for half a dozen comfrey offsets but also for a supply of ointment, cream, tablets, tea and flour; and thus fortified, I shall hope to face this winter of discontent.

Woad Show

Guardian readers are in general reputed to be knowledgeable and nice — an assessment amply confirmed by correspondence which followed my expressed wish to rediscover woad on my allotment, and be reassured that Queen Bess had been unjust in her Tudor condemnation of its "noysome savour."

Mrs Jocelyn Jackson wrote to say that woad *(Isatis tinctoria)* is alive and well in Newcastle-upon-Tyne; flowering in her garden, in fact "with delicate golden flower-heads reminiscent of cow-parsley." Mr J.H. Holness also has woad growing in his Cheshire garden, front and back, approaching six feet in height at the back. "The plant," he says, "is by no means malodorous, but the process involves steeping in water with lime, and this could be the stage to give offence." Woad, as a plant, is therefore respectable, even if the Ancient Britons who dyed their bodies blue with it were not; and this gives the go-ahead to a staid plot-holder like myself.

Mrs Marston of our local University Botanic Gardens has now introduced me to blooming woad and other dye plants. She has also introduced me to Mrs Dawn MacLeod's valuable and lively *Book of Herbs* which, with its short chapter "Dyeing with Plants," will fill some of the gaps in my newly acquired know-how. *A History of Dye Textiles* by Stuart Robinson, recommended by the librarian at Kew, will help anyone who wishes to take dyeing seriously.

Mrs MacLeod says woad was cultivated as a dye plant at Tewkesbury, Wisbech and Glastonbury, the "Glas" of the last being Celtic for grey-blue, as glastum was Roman for woad, both the dye and the plant.

Woad seeds may be sown in June but the plants will not bloom till next year. Nor will mine, sown in May; and if they are anti-Ancient British enough to fail me, Mr

Holness promises me some self-sown seedlings. I look forward, therefore, to the company of woad on my plot, though I have reservations about exploiting it for home dyeing purposes. Woad processing, as I have come to understand it, seems a bit off-putting.

You pick the leaves, dry them in the sun, crush them into paste, expose this paste to air and fermentation, break it and form it into cakes, then crush these to powder, moisten and ferment a second time till the stuff becomes hot and steaming, to cool finally and fill the air with the scent of ammonia — cause enough, I would say, for Queen Bess to banish it from within a radius of five miles of her royal residences. The two-month-long process was once a craft that went in families (often nomadic ones) and was handed down from one generation to the next.

"I daresay you will discover," writes Mrs Jackson, "a vast underground movement of home-dyers, especially among *Guardian* readers." Courses run by the Northumberland College of Agriculture are, it seems, attended by enthusiasts from far afield, including Scotland. One begins to foresee a return to cottage industries and to the general use of home-grown and home-processed plant dyes — which, Mrs MacLeod says, have a greater richness, subtlety and "life" than the synthetics. Before long we may be planting up our allotments and gardens with dye plants among the mint and parsley, as the New England colonists once did.

Mr Jim Shalleron of North London faults me for failing to discover some natural plant juices for "fixing" dyes. "The Ancients," he says, "had no chemist's shop in which to buy alum mordant." Had they not? *Chambers Encyclopaedia* says: "Alum was known to the Egyptians, Greeks and Romans," and my friend who knows China well says the Ancient Chinese knew it too.

There are, however, some natural dyes that don't need a mordant. Mr Joe Davies of Bishopbriggs, Glasgow, in a most informative letter with samples, names one of these — the lichen Crotal *(Parmelia saxatales)* — which he says

166

is still scraped from the rocks on Harris, the depth of colour depending on the amount of lichen used and the length time of boiling.

An Indian doctor friend tells that at the February spring festival in Northern India, the girls dye their white saris yellow, just for the event, outshining the flowering mustard of the surrounding fields. Afterwards they wash out the due, or allow it to fade gracefully and evenly. So why should we bother about mordants? We bother too much about too many things, instead of going into the garden to prepare a dye-plant bed — with a space for Soapwort *(Saponaria officinalis)* for cleaning raw wool.

Garlic

Garlic, though still not altogether accepted in the politest circles, finds a happy home on an allotment. Among the ancients, I understand, the upper classes of sweeter breath disdained to touch it, preferring to feed it to their slaves for added strength, to their soldiers for greater courage, and to their criminals to purge them of criminality.

Personally, I rely on my own small garlic bed not only for these attributes but for an inexpensive year-round kitchen supply. My bulbs are for the most part the progeny of a chance purchase from a village greengrocer some years ago. They are anonymous as to provenance but nicely white-skinned when sun-ripened in the autumn and hung up airily in easily accessible bunches.

With more caution, you can buy the bulbs from a reliable seed merchant to separate the so-called "cloves" (up to a dozen to a bulb and easily detachable) and plant these with nose-end uppermost somewhat shallowly about six inches apart, preferably in a light rich soil, in a sunny position in February or March. Or you can sow garlic seed when the weather gets warmer.

In recent years, with gifts from friends, I have made small exotic additions to my garlic endeavours — a few Greek "cloves" from Chalcis, where Aristotle died, and a few from Portugal. I now await a specimen from Dalmatia, where the Roman Emperor Diocletian set a good example (which I never regret having followed) when he retired to the country to cultivate cabbages — and doubtless a garlic patch as well, since he was of lowly birth and possibly of unsweetened breath.

Garlic in the garden is accommodatingly tough, tolerant and untemperamental — bothered by weeds more than by other forms of neglect. You harvest it when the leaves have withered, which happens in late July from an autumn planting and a month or two later if you plant in

March, and if on this account you overlook any bulbs (as I did last year) they will sprout up in clumps and you can dig them up in the spring and offer them to garlic-deprived friends for separate and single transplantation.

I rather think that garlic is obliging enough to allow itself to be planted or transplanted at almost any time. Certainly if you are of a forgetful nature or suffer from cold fingers in February you can take the (very slight) rick of planting your cloves immediately after lifting the bulbs, and inviting them to overwinter for you. You will be able to clear the crop in time for a sowing of spring cabbages.

Garlic also has side-effects to offer the gardener or allotmenteer. Its presence is said to drive away moles — and certainly I have had to "talpaic" invasion since I introduced garlic to my plot. It is said to drive away other pests as well, and I could believe this too. Some claim that a garlic spray on cabbages will put the cabbage butterfly off the scient: and that a jet of the spray at ground level will do for the cabbage root fly.

Some say garlic intensifies the perfume of nearby roses; this too I could accept because my own allotment roses are but a yard or so from my garlic territory, and are (allowing for personal bias) richly scented.

From the health point of view, it is open to us all to turn to garlic as a ready source of help in time of trouble, encouraged by the knowledge that health-conscious gorillas seek to set up home where wild garlic grows.

In herbalist terms, it is diaphoretic (promotes perspiration), diuretic, expectorant and stimulant; it aids digestion, keeps the lining of the stomach healthy, is anti-cholesterol, and has antiseptic and cooling properties both internally and externally. It also contributes an appetising culinary smell and flavour by the merest smearing of a bruised clove on a salad dish, or its inclusion in soups and casseroles.

It could also lead a man to fortune. In 1973 I read that a Lee Valley grower got a £3,000 return per acre when he experimented with garlic-growing on a commercial scale;

for myself, however, being born without ambition and devoid of all business acumen, I throw out the idea for others to snatch up.

I am indebted to Yann Lovelock *(The Vegetable Book)* for the intriguing information that European gardeners are beginning to be interested in fragrant-flowered garlic *(Allium odorum),* a species which grows wild in China where they eat the bulb raw and use the flower as a pot-herb. I must certainly go in search of it.

Rootful Abundance

To put down roots is good advice, not least in the vegetable plot. You can eat them fresh in summer and autumn, and store them for winter and spring. Carrots are difficult on our allotment, and in consequence we favour the parsnip, encourage the beetroot, and intend to show more partiality to the turnip and the swede.

Take the parsnip. It is relatively easy to grow and stands stalwartly by you throughout the bleak midwinter. My wife likes it as a nourishing vegetable and potato substitute whilst I make it a mainstay for home-made white wine. It can remain in the ground until March (or February if the winter is mild), at which time, being a biennial plant, it sends up new growth, using for itself the food which you had thought to be yours.

There are nowadays more varieties of parsnip to choose from. Sutton's "Improved Hollow Crown" and Dobie's "Exhibition" have long roots. One of our plot-holders dug out a specimen five feet long: mine snapped off somewhere about two spits deep and laid me low with lumbago. This year, therefore, I shall switch to the smaller-rooted sorts. "Avonresister" is one such, and is said to be pleasant-flavoured and canker-resistant. "Offenbaum" is another. Suttons advertise their new "White gem" as having "considerable tolerance to canker" and being a heavy cropper on all soil types.

Parsnips, nevertheless, do not like an acid soil. A well-dug, deep, rich, light soil, not newly manured, is ideal for growing good specimens without forked roots, especially if you rake in a little general fertiliser a few days before sowing. Usual advice is to sow the seed thinly in February and March, but I have found a second sowing in April or May to be more successful: its products are the ones that see us through the winter, improved and sweetened by frost. Nor do I follow the somewhat perfectionist advice of thinning out to one foot between plants and a foot and a half between rows. Preferring more and smaller parsnips to fewer and larger ones, I leave less space in both directions. In any case, there is recent evidence that smaller roots sown at a later date are less prone to canker damage — provided you are careful not to catch the root tops when hoeing. (Maggots of the carrot fly can be a bigger nuisance.)

After the parsnip (with or without butter) we render thanks for the benefits of beetroot. This needs much the same soil preparation and culture as the parsnip, but the seed should be sown even more thinly (each seed produces several plants) and not till the soil is warm. A thin dressing of common salt along the drill at sowing time is said to be a good thing, if the kitchen can spare it.

The round types of beet, like "Early Bunch" and "Boltardy" are good for early pulling, while the long types, like "Cheltenham Green-top" are best for storage — if you have the discipline and space to store them, in sand or straw, away from frosts. For our part we usually find, at lifting time in October, that we boil, bottle and gourmandise on our beetroot until there is none left to store. This year, however, I mean to make a trial final sowing of the round type in July and leave it in the ground till needed. Suttons "Gold Beet" is a dual-purpose type, the roots being at their best when young and the leaves eaten as spinach.

Both parsnips and beet (and indeed root crops generally) abhor dry spells, which check growth. At such times one should grab the opportunity after a welcome shower, to sprinkle a general fertiliser alongside the row and cover this with a mulch of compost to keep in the moisture.

The turnip can also make a change in summer and fill a gap in winter. My July-sown "Snowball" variety seems aptly named both for size and hue, but a fellow plot-holder recommends "Golden Ball" for taste and for storing.

The swede I am about to grow for the first time, having noticed in the greengrocers the price per pound of this enjoyable (especially with haggis) vegetable. Sutton's "Chignecto," bred for its resistance to clubroot, I shall sow in May, and thus hope to escape foliage mildew. "Purple Top" is advertised as quick-growing and excellent for eating young as well as for winter storage. This is another vegetable obliging enough to stay in the cold ground until wanted.

And that's not all. The avoirdupoidal Winter Radish may also be sown in July, lightly thinner, and left in the ground till wanted. Only in the blackest of winter weather does it welcome a warm covering of straw. Roots weighing one whole pound are not unknown, so that, needless to say, some slicing or shreding is required for its use in salads. For size it certainly puts out of countenance its spring cousin.

For the connoisseur there is also the root salsify. When sown in April and thinned to about six inches apart, this smaller root of "vegetable oyster" can be used from November onwards, boiled, sliced and quickly fried in butter, I shall also sow a sample of Scorzonera "Russian Giant" to savour the reported delicate flavour of this black-skinned root, which must be scalded, scraped and boiled in salted water till tender.

Parsley: The Good Companion

Almost nothing on an allotment need be wasted — especially if you regard most of your weeds as vegetables or herbs. My winter covering of chickweed could at a pinch be cooked for spinach, as they did in the old days; and all those creeping rhizomes of couch grass which I uprooted so easily in the soil conditions of last autumn could, with more wisdom, have been cleaned and used for health giving tea.

Not until a few weeks ago, greatly daring, did I for the first time make a brew of dried comfrey leaves, bought two years ago and pushed away in a plastic bag. I found the infusion as pleasant as china tea.

After this discovery I naturally hurried to the allotment for reassurance that all was well with my own comfrey plants, left out there in the cold, and used by me in the summer as a green manure for their potash content. But in looking for the comfrey, my attention was diverted to a few surviving rosettes of parsley, vividly green amid the encircling snow, and peering at me reproachfully for failing to give them some winter protection.

Clearly, I have been taking my parsley too much for granted, sowing it in spring, tiring of waiting for it to germinate, planting something else on top, and then finding odd rewarding patches thereabouts to keep us in good supply. Henceforth, however, I shall treat my parsley with a proper respect.

It is a biennial which may be regarded as a perennial (if you pull off the flower stalks as they grow) but is perhaps best treated as an annual, by making a succession of sowings in spring and summer, and using the leaves while young. A July sowing to overwinter — as I am learning to my cost — will appreciate some protection from northern blasts — preferably, they say, at the foot of a south-facing wall.

Most of this year's catalogues offer a choice of either two or three varieties (excluding Hamburg Parsley, which is really a root crop, and French Parsley, which is related to celery). Marshalls of Wisbech, however, offer no fewer than six — Fenland Green, Dark Green Winter, Moss Curled, Lincoln Green, Bravous and Triplex. The first they claim to be slow to run to seed, the second to stand well in winter, and the rest to be of proved worth. I have sent for them all, determined to do my own bit of parsley experiment and research. I certainly intend to make some parsley wine, for which I shall need about a pound of parsley to the gallon, picked in June, with two or three pounds of sugar and a general-purpose yeast. It is said to qualify as a delicious "hock."

Allotment Tipples

One day in September I bottled six gallons of gooseberry wine made in June from my allotment gooseberries and four gallons of elderflower with acknowledgements to the allotment hedge. I corked the bottles with soaked and sterilised corks, sealed them on top with candle wax, stored them in the covered alcove at the back of the garage which is my wine cellar, and in the middle of the night we were wakened by an explosion: one of the bottles had blown up.

In the morning, mopping up and gathering up the pieces, I detected some trespassing yeast on the fragment of the bottle which had been its base. This is a warning to all home wine-makers to rack wine carefully and stabilise it with camden tablets before bottling; or alternatively, if you prefer sparkling gooseberry wine, vying with champagne itself, to bottle it in strong bottles with the corks well tied down — preferably in old champagne bottles thrown out in your direction.

Home-made wines can be a useful allotment sideline. You can make them from vegetables and herbs as well as from fruit and flowers. Take parsley for instance. The books recommend parsley wine and give recipes for it. So last spring I sowed samples of seven different varieties, and by July all seven - looking pretty much alike to the untutored eye — were asking to be cropped. I gathered one pound (or say a quart pot full and lightly pressed down) and with about three pounds of sugar made a gallon of wine. I used champagne yeast because that is what the man in the local wine-making shop recommended.

"Parsley wine is very good for rheumatism," he said; and when I reacted a little doubtfully, he added, "We... helps you to suffer it more gladly, let's say."

Not having made parsley wine before, I am not yet in a position to recommend, either for rheumatism or for bucolic enjoyment, but after dipping a drinking straw into the fermenting jar at three months and sampling it, I have high hopes. Doubters can always, at the outset, add white wine concentrate to this home-made hippocras for better assurance. And they can use all-purpose yeast, I understand, with confidence.

My fingers are similarly crossed over my bubbling broad bean brew — another experimental gallon. This autumn I left a considerable number of pods on the plants to dry off, blacken, and offer their seeds for next season. Of these, when gathered, I saved only the largest and most favoured beans, turning over the small or ill-shapen ones to wine-making.

There were about three pounds of these, though less, I"m sure, would do, especially if you were to use some white wine concentrate as well with an easy conscience. You bring the tough hard beans to the boil, simmer for an hour, allow to cool, and strain off the liquid for your wine, using a German yeast. The residue of still whole beans may be used for the compost heap or for the table, according to taste or prejudice.

I have come to think of the first half of the year as the time for white wine-making. Even the blood-red early beets make a golden wine — and a nice one too. And rhubarb wine should be made, if at all, by the end of June. Autumn is for red wine — blackberry and elderberry especially, My Oregon Thornless blackberries did exceptionally well this year, and all that were not required for some delicious and subtly flavoured jelly went into wine.

Root vegetables can make very acceptable wine — particularly parsnips, which are best left in the ground for frosting and taken up for wine-making in the New Year. For root wines you scrub hard (but don't peel), dice or slice (but not too small), bring to the boil and simmer till tender (but not till mushy), strain off the liquid for wine and, if you have the appetite, eat the vegetables. All the books give you a parsnip wine recipe because — if you can manage to keep it for a year — it is so special.

The Jerusalem artichoke, I understand, also makes a good wine, though I have yet to try it. I did, however, make some potato wine three years ago. "Don't touch it!" warned an authority on amyl, isobutyl and propyl alcohols at the time. "People have been blinded by drinking new potato wine. Don't touch it for at least three years." I shall play safe and leave mine for four.

Luckily I have safer vintages in my cellar and three rows of parsnips of the allotment waiting for my next wine-making festival — an occasion, alas, when my wife can't stand the heat and keeps out of the kitchen.

All in the End
is Harvest?

This Blessed Plot

At what age is it wise to pack up gardening? As a mid-octogenarian this concerns me. Friends offer conflicting advice. There are those who say that it's best to stop and accept the inevitable. Others, like Leslie, an ardent allotmenteer, think otherwise. You should keep going, he says, in spite of aches, pains, and a propensity to trip and fall, until you are reduced to a square yard or so of manageable plot.

Leslie took it upon himself last year to reclaim my remaining half-plot from the state of rampant enveloping nature to which it had rapidly succumbed during an illness. His volunteered help was generous and unstinting. It involved many hours of hard labour. I felt constrained therefore to follow his advice and to accept help with an easy conscience.

There was, however, a problem. I had, of necessity, parted with my old Morris Minor which had not only carried me to my beloved rural plot but had acted as garden shed while working there.

Fortunately for me, the transport difficulty was overcome when Len, my next door neighbour and a confessed non gardener, offered to drive me to the allotments on suitable Saturday mornings with a flask of coffee and tin full of biscuits to consume at half-time, sitting beside the Autumn Bliss raspberries. He was to work while I would sit and instruct him.

And so, happily, it befell, to the satisfaction of all concerned. Sheila continued to mow and trim my serpentining pathways with elegant precision, while Leslie kept an eye on things generally; and to avoid a second slipping into iniquity, Len dug. His wife Jennifer became a willing martyr to hand-weeding and gave good advice.

That was last year.

This year has been delightfully different. Len has taken retirement. He has become a fully-fledged allotmenteer,

181

going to the plot almost daily, sometimes twice a day. He enjoys his new-found freedom, the fresh air, companionship, controlled exercise, tranquility, and all the gifts that allotmenteering bestows in our pleasant rural setting, far from the madding crowd's often ignoble strife. My present status is therefore that of a sometimes garden-chair plot holder, accepting with gratitude the help of others.

My main role this year is to stay at home and sow seeds in pots and trays with benefit of a cold frame. When they are ready, Len and Jennifer take these seedlings and young plants to the plot, transplant them, and return the empties in a continuing horticultural shuttle service. This works well, except when beetroot and lettuce take to bolting.

Thus we share fresh vegetables and fruit, the welcome produce of this new regime and division of labour. Len hungers for horticultural knowledge when he is not constructing wooden-framed, netted cages against marauders, — rabbits and pigeons mostly, and small bird raiders in the soft fruit season. Jennifer is an adept with soft fruit — gooseberry syllabub a speciality.

Moreover, I join in the regular Sunday joint at Jennifer's table with rarely fewer than half a dozen allotment vegetables to choose from, expertly cooked and served with appropriate sauces.

But I still miss those days when I used to make an early summer morning visit to the allotment to see the sun rise against the dawning sky, and watch the world awaken. And it is now Len — not I — who greets our resident tame robin, awaiting his arrival.

Plot Bound No More

It is sad to lose your grip on an allotment you have held for almost a quarter of a century, and equally doleful to relinquish the 35-year-old Morris Minor which has served valiantly for transport and as a mobile allotment shed.

It was even more melancholy-inducing to arrive one morning at the allotments to find that my Plot 11 had become 11A and 11B — the B not indicating a downgrading so much as my area of soft fruits, herbs, flowers, and wild corners of uninhibited weeds, still manageable by me. The A could stand for arable, demanding industrious digging by its new and younger tenant.

But I miss my old willow green Minor badly, for all its acquired dents and bruises. Its boisterous running noise was somehow comforting. I rejoice, however, that it has a good home with Antony, a car-oriented enthusiast who before his recent marriage used to live with his parents next door to me, from which close proximity he had coveted my banger for years. He would have driven it away the moment I offered it had I not pleaded for time and a less hasty goodbye; and when it had gone it left behind emptiness, not only in the garage.

Guilt feelings assailed me. I had not given it the care and attention it deserved. I had never washed it but left it out in the rain for its ablutions. It was grubby and quite noticeably neglected; but Antony preferred to see this as character.

He and Ruth, his young wife, gave it a thorough spring clean with soap and water, inside and out, leather upholstery, chromium number plate and all. When they removed a washed seat and propped it to dry against a wall, somewhat to their surprise, I gather, they witnessed an escaping mouse — a native of my allotment perhaps, but now a fugitive.

Mice have always used the allotment hut as a winter squat, surviving it seems on chewed items of left-behind clothing scarves, gloves, and discarded *Guardian* newspapers which they chewed to shreds.

I shall miss the mice. I was happy to give them a winter home. I shall also miss the resident and always welcoming robin, the voracious thieving rabbits, the bold blackbirds, the odd visiting pheasant or pair of partridges, a passing hedgehog and overhead hovering hawk.

Parting will be such sweet sorrow, but ultimately I realise that I shall have to bid goodbye to this good earth and blessed plot but with, I hope, some returning visits to refresh allotment acquaintances and watch vegetative progress.

I shall take away enduring memories, happy and sad, of storm and flood, crisp frost and earth scorching drought, gale and pervading peace; of companionship, healthy air, and the therapeutic open space of our enclave behind a Capability Brown belt of trees, far enough removed from houses and madding crowds. I shall remember the Old Departed — Old Bob who, in spite of irritating war wounds, filled my early allotment days with friendly greetings, cheerful chat, and sound advice. There was Charles of the model plot, producing high-class vegetables. He introduced himself to me, offering a handsome cauliflower; a cup for competition commemorates him at the local show.

Then there was the young professional gardener with the plot next to mine who improved my horticultural education until he left for Bermuda and success. And I shan't forget poor old Ralph who at the time lumbered his way heavily towards his plot speaking to no one but swearing quietly to himself at life's ill treatment.

Above all there was Nelson, now almost 90, whose allotmenteering was suddenly stopped by a stroke from which he slowly recovers and complains only of corns. A true countryman of the old school, he retired and became my plot associate, and the arch enemy of weeds.

I can still keep going, pottering around the house this winter while indulging in windowsill and airing -cupboard gardening with no one to complain about spilled compost on carpets.

From Unwins I have a packet of blue Tibetan Poppy (Meconopsis betonicifolia) with instructions for improved germination resulting from a decade of research in their laboratories, which reverses the more usual procedure.

You sow in a small pot in a warm place (68°F), leave for two weeks, then move to the main part of your fridge (c. 40°F). Ten to 14 days later, germination is expected to begin and you check regularly, pricking out the seedlings as they appear and giving them light in a warm place (65-70°F). I shall hope to follow instructions to the letter to confirm the patient work of Alison Mulvaney and others at Histon, Cambridge. Full instructions appear on the packet.

The Editors

David Crouch is Professor of Cultural Geography at Anglia University, and Visiting Professor, Karlstad University, Sweden. He has contributed to many academic journals and books on geography, leisure and landscape and has assisted with a number of television programmes on allotments. Together with Colin Ward, David Crouch wrote *The Allotment: Its Landscape and Culture* (Five Leaves).

Martin Stott is an organic allotment-holder and campaigner. He is a trustee of the Elderstubbs Site in Oxford. Martin Stott's previous books include *Spilling the Beans* (HarperCollins), *Beyond Isolation* (ICOM) and *The Nuclear Controversy* (TCPA). Martin Stott has organised and contributed to several exhibitions of allotment photographs.

Also Available from Five Leaves

One Woman's Plot
by Geraldine Kilbride

One Woman's Plot is an allotment diary of a downwardly mobile middle-aged woman, who, knowing nothing about growing anything, casually takes on the challenge of two allotments. Her newfound hobby verges on being a few carrots short of a full harvest.

This quirky account of taming a small temperate rainforest, in the London Borough of Richmond, may not inspire experienced gardeners but will give them something to chuckle over once the real gardening business of the day is done.

Geraldine Kilbride used to be a high-flyer in sales and marketing... she gardens in London.

116 pages, 0 907123 86 4 (pbk), £6.00

The Allotment: Its Landscape and Culture
by David Crouch and Colin Ward

The standard work on allotments, covering everything apart from horticulture, includes a new introduction outlining the current statistics of allotment use and changes in practice - including the increase in allotment holding by women and younger people. *The Allotment* has spawned four television programmes with another in preparation.

320 pages, 0 907123 91 0 (pbk), £10.99

"...to all of you, I recommend that classic, The Allotment"
The Observer

"Learned and literary, Crouch and Ward are like Orwellian socialists in their defence of small, important rights"
The Guardian

"...a wise and stimulating book"
Sunday Telegraph

Five Leaves' titles are available from bookshops,
or, postfree, from Five Leaves,
PO Box 81, Nottingham NG5 4ER

ALSO AVAILABLE FROM FIVE LEAVES

The Allotment: Its Landscape and Culture
David Crouch and Colin Ward

A new edition of this classic book on allotment life, history and culture. **The Allotment** includes everything you need to know about allotments apart from horticulture. **The Allotment** has spawned no less than four television programmes, the last being **The Plot** on Channel 4. This new edition updates the struggle to hold onto allotment land and details the latest research on allotment use.

...to all of you, I recommend that classic, The Allotment
(The Observer)

Learned and literary, Crouch and Ward are like Orwellian socialists in their defence of small, important rights
(The Guardian)

David Crouch is Professor of Cultural Geography at Anglia University and the author of many articles in academic journals. Colin Ward has written numerous books on the environment, planning and housing.

326 pages : 0 907123 91 0 : £10.99

Postfree from Five Leaves, PO Box 81, Nottingham NG5 4ER.